MEXICO BEFORE CORTEZ: ART, HISTORY, LEGEND
REVISED EDITION
BY
IGNACIO BERNAL

TRANSLATION BY
WILLIS BARNSTONE

*With Additional English-Language Material
By Ignacio Bernal*

Anchor Books
Anchor Press/Doubleday
Garden City, New York
1975

Mexico before Cortez: Art, History, Legend
was published in Spanish as
Tenochtitlán en Una Isla

The Anchor Books edition is the same as the Dolphin
Books edition, which was the first publication of *Tenochtitlán en Una Isla* in English in 1963.

Anchor Books Edition: 1973

Revised Edition: 1975

MEXICO BEFORE CORTEZ

IGNACIO BERNAL is Director of the National Museum of Anthropology and Subdirector of the National Institute of Anthropology of Mexico. He received his M.A. and Ph.D. in Anthropological Science, specializing in archaeology, from the University of Mexico, and has been Professor of Anthropology at the National University of Mexico and Director of the Department of Anthropology at Mexico City College. Dr. Bernal has served as Cultural Attaché of the Mexican Embassy in France, as Permanent Delegate to UNESCO, and was President of the XXXV Congress of Americanists. As a lecturer on Mexican art and culture, he has given conferences in the United States and Europe. His books on Mexican archaeology and art have been published in Mexico, France, and the United States. He is a member of the Academia Mexicana de Historia.

WILLIS BARNSTONE is Associate Professor of Spanish and Comparative Literature at Indiana University. Born in Lewiston, Maine, he received his M.A. from Columbia and his Ph.D. from Yale. He is the author of three books of poetry and has translated the work of the contemporary Spanish poet Antonio Machado, as well as plays of Lope de Vega and Calderon de la Barca. Mr. Barnstone is editor of an anthology of contemporary European poetry, editor and translator of a volume of Greek lyric poetry and a volume of Sappho's poems, and has translated a novel from modern Greek. In 1961 Mr. Barnstone was a Guggenheim fellow in Spain, where he completed a critical study of Antonio Machado.

CONTENTS

PLATES

TEXT DRAWINGS

MEXICO BEFORE CORTEZ

PROLOGUE

Suddenly, they came to the end of their long ascent. Starting at the sea, their march had taken them to the pass between the volcanoes. Now on the high snow, the men of steel on their heraldic horses looked down upon an extraordinary spectacle. There in the distance, far below, was a broad valley. In the center were silver lakes, and on islands and the shores rose the lofty roofs of temples resting on massive pyramids. Forests and violet and yellow farmlands brightened the plain in those magical days of Mexican autumn. It was the Valley of Tenochtitlán (today Mexico City), whose great promise led Cortez and his soldiers to enter Anahuac. For the first time in history, a Western man looked upon this admirable landscape diffused in the afternoon haze. The leader's eyes glowed as he studied the prize which lay on the plain.

"And after we saw so many cities and towns built on the water, and other cities on the surrounding land, and that straight and level causeway which entered the city, we were amazed and said that it was like the enchanted places recounted in Amadis de Gaula, because of the great towers and buildings which grew out of the water, all made of stone and mortar, and some of our soldiers even asked whether what they saw was not a dream, and do not wonder that I write in this way, for there is so much to ponder over in all these things that I do not know how to describe them. We saw things never heard or even dreamed about before."

The soldier-chronicler Bernal Díaz del Castillo continues: "On another morning . . . we were walking along the causeway, which is eight paces wide and runs directly into Mexico City, and which I think does not bend at all, and although it is very broad it was crowded with innumerable people, some entering Mexico City and others leaving and those Indians who came out to see us coming, and there were so many that we could not go around them; they crammed the towers and temples and canoes which filled the lagoon, and it was not surprising since they had never seen horses or men such as we. And as we saw such wonderful things, we were speechless—was what appeared before us real?—for great cities rose from the land and the lagoon, and we saw the water crowded with canoes, and many bridges at intervals along the causeway, and before us was the great city of Mexico."

A few days later, Moctezuma, the Tlacatecuhtli, received the Spaniards in a historic ceremony resplendent with colored feathers and gifts, and he lodged them in his father's palace. After a short, prudent wait, during which Cortez foresaw an easy triumph, the admiring leader asked to go up to the great temple. Moctezuma accompanied him, anxious to avoid any sacrilege. And on reaching the top, the lord of Mexico "took him by the hand and told him to look at his great city and all the other cities on the water and the many other towns along the land around the lagoon; and if he had not seen his great plaza well, from there he could see it much better. And so we stood looking about us, for that huge and cursed temple was so high that it dominated everything; and from there we saw the three causeways that led into the city. . . . And we saw the fresh water that came down from the hills of Chapultepec, supplying the city, and we saw those three causeways and the bridges which crossed them at intervals, under which the lagoon water flowed back and forth; and we gazed at a great multitude of canoes in that great lagoon, some coming in with food and provisions and others going out with cargoes of merchandise; and we saw in that great city and in all the other cities on the water that one could go from one house to another only by means of wooden drawbridges or by canoes; and we saw cues and temples built like towers and fortresses and all gleaming white, a marvel to behold, and flat-roofed houses, and along the causeway other small towers and temples that were like fortresses. And after we had looked carefully and pondered over what we had seen, we looked again at the great plaza and the crowds of people in it, some buying, others selling, and the booming hubbub of voices and words could be heard a league away, and there were soldiers among us who had been in many parts of the world, in Constantinople and in Italy and Rome, and they said that they never had seen such crowds of people in such a large and well-proportioned plaza."

From skyscrapers along the Paseo de la Reforma, today's visitor can still see the immutable mountains and the extraordinary valley, but the lakes which were so important in ancient history have now disappeared, and chimney smoke now stains the diaphanous air. It is futile to look for the ruins of an Indian temple among the buildings of the metropolis. By the end of the sixteenth century, there was not a single monument of ancient Tenochtitlán left standing. Only through our imagination and the infrequent archaeological explorations can we reconstruct the spectacle which Bernal Díaz del Castillo described to us in his splendid prose.

How and why did Tenochtitlán become what it was? To understand this we must go back many centuries and study the little we know of this valley and its lakes. Let us recall that the Mexica represent only a façade of the ancient history of Mexico. A brilliant façade, warlike and religious, cruel and mystical, behind which is hidden, as in Egypt, a long, relevant past. It was a past dating back thousands of years, already forgotten by the time Spain opened up the ports of America to Europe, a past in which numerous peoples and civilizations followed one upon the other, each a victim of its own insanities, and destroyed by the ever-present barbarians.

The history we shall relate took place in a setting of fantastic beauty. The immense valley, at 7244 feet above sea level, lies below a circle of mountains some of which reach an altitude of 15,500 feet (Plate 1). Four other valleys surround it, Puebla and Toluca to the east and west,

Teotlalpam and the plains of Morelos to the north and south. The volcanoes gradually became extinct, some in the historical era. Only great, unchanging Popocatepetl, like a kindly grandfather, still contemplates the human anthill. Lazily, it draws on its pipe and now and then hurls up puffs of smoke without frightening anyone.

Fig. 1 The lakes in different periods: (1) In the times of the Man of Tepexpam; (2) In the Mexica period; (3) Around 1800; (4) In 1889. Now they have almost entirely disappeared. [Taken from Schilling, Elizabeth, Die "schwimmenden Gärten" von Xochimilco, Kiel, 1938, fig. 3.]

In the Indian period, the mountains were covered with forests that also stretched out across a large part of the flatland. The remaining plain lay below the waters of the lagoons which, although joined, retained their separate identity. There was the fresh water lagoon of Xochimilco, the salty lagoon of Texcoco, and the others. . . .

These lakes both produced a great civilization and swallowed it up afterward, and today they continue to cause the modern city to sink in its own mud. These marvelous lakes on whose banks the first man appeared in Mesoamerica, lakes that formed the water and earth on which an entire ancient world flourished thanks to their fertile, irrigated shores, lakes among whose islands one would become famous with time—Tenochtitlán—these lakes are the creators and destroyers of the people they created. Generously, they gave everything to man, only to reclaim all from him later in the quagmire. Now they are dry, yet take their revenge on the city which annihilated them by making it into a ship that is slowly sinking.

It is then on these shores that the long history, whose last chapter we have just read, took place. In this book we shall try to explain the episodes through which man of the Central Plateau of Mexico passed as he developed from his most humble beginnings to Mexica splendor.

FOREWORD

The aim of this small volume is simply to outline the
history that made Tenochtitlán what it was, and at the
same time to mention some of the main events and the
spirit that brought them about. The numerous quotations,
especially from Indian authors, are for the sake of sketch-
ing the ideas—so difficult for us to grasp—around which the
ancient Mexican civilization developed and which are the
key to many events. The anecdotes may seem frivolous but
apart from being amusing, they help to recapture the spiritual picture. That is why I have included so many. Like
the text, the illustrations seek only to evoke the past and
are placed among the various themes as they arise, with
no break in the text for specific reference to each one.
Many have the merit of being previously unpublished,
though use of others that are commonplace could not be
avoided. I have included neither notes nor bibliography.

My account could have been quite different, for one can
draw various interpretations, perhaps equally valid, for almost every archaeological or historical fact. The reader will
notice many changes between this edition and the first one.
In almost fifteen years our knowledge of this field has advanced considerably. New explorations and new studies on
various aspects of the subject have obliged me to change
my opinions and therefore to modify what I want to say
in a book of this type. I repeat that it is an impressionistic
volume that endeavors to give a spiritual perception rather
than to describe in detail or depth the ancient civilization
whose indelible traces still mark the Mexico of today.

I have made use not only of the old authors but also
of the works by our contemporaries, especially those of
Wigberto Jiménez Moreno, always so generous and who

I am sure will forgive my frequent misuse of his excellent ideas. He and my wife Sofía have been my principal victims; it is therefore only right that this book be dedicated to them both.

I. THE ORIGINS

Only recently has archaeology begun to fathom the mystery. Some groups of human beings, some ruins, some styles of art, the sole testaments of vanished peoples, have been drawn out of oblivion. Excavations have led us to move back the beginnings of American history beyond what was formerly believed, and in the Valley of Mexico we can now mention dates going back to many millennia before Christ.

In this period the banks and marshes of the lakes were covered with vegetation. It was an ideal situation favoring the development of a varied fauna, which in turn provided excellent food for the huge pachyderms, mammoths, and mastodons or ancient elephants that roamed the area. The bison, American horse, bear, camel, and various other animals inhabited the region. They were the kings. Man—so far as we know—emerged only at that moment, and with him began the great drama of history.

At the beginning he was simple and primitive. Small, hungry groups of nomadic hunters came to the valleys. There—who knows after what ordeals—they hunted down the great wild animals. By burning the dry grass, they drove elephants toward the marshes where they killed them as soon as the beasts were caught in the mud. They would cut them up and usually eat them on the spot. It was a splendid banquet that lasted several days, and they ate as much as possible as a measure against future hunger. Primitive man—like the gourmet of today—did not mind consuming aged meat. The leftover scraps from these hunts give us the first sign of human presence in Mexico.

Several discoveries a few miles from the capital have enabled us to make this statement. One of them in Santa

Isabel Iztapan consists of the skeleton of an elephant that undoubtedly was killed by men. An obsidian knife point was still attached to a rib and a number of implements were found scattered among the bones. These objects that were used to kill or cut up the animal represent a technical development comparable to that of paleolithic Europe. Although a few findings made in the nineteenth century already suggested it, in Iztapan we have for the first time in Mexico certain proof that man lived contemporaneously with animals now extinct.

A short distance away another discovery revealed no animals or implements but man himself: a man who perhaps perished during a hunt, killed by an elephant, or else one simply buried in the mud of the marshes. This "first Mexican," whom we know as the "Man of Tepexpan," was five feet, seven inches tall, approximately sixty years old, with a mesocephalic skull, and his blood was probably of group A. He belongs to the same race as and resembles the future inhabitants of the region. This remote ancestor, along with his companions and his women and children, led the rough life of a nomadic hunter. He made his own stone utensils, which have come down to us, as well as objects of perishable material that we shall never know. He possessed the *atlatl*, spear, and stone knife, he had learned to use fire. The dog, that faithful animal which it is said has civilized man, appeared in the Valley of Tehuacán only when agriculture was becoming important. Thus the saying is not so inexact since the dog accompanied his master during the latter's rise to civilization. We have no earlier traces although it is certain that dogs came to America with the first immigrants. Very recent discoveries in the Peñón, at Santa María Aztahuacan and at San Vicente Chicoloapan, among others, have confirmed the presence of man in the Central Highlands since at least fourteen thousand years ago. Excavations still in progress at Tlapacoya suggest even more ancient dates.

Later, but still several millennia before Christ, perhaps because of constant killings by hungry man or because of climatic changes, the great "antediluvian" animals disappeared from the earth. This must have radically changed the economic life of the primitive hunter. His hunting was reduced to trapping smaller animals or those which could be eaten in a single mouthful. From then on began what was to become a common trait of American societies: meat was not the basis of their diet but rather a luxury item. Plants had to fill in the gap. But in their natural state plants can only partially succeed in this task. Man could no longer be satisfied with what untended nature supplied him. He had to aid her, spur her on, and later transform her. And so the agricultural age began.

Determining how and when corn was first grown in America has been one of the problems over which scholars have spilled great quantities of ink. Geographers and botanists, archaeologists and linguists, as well as many other specialists, have studied the problem from diverse angles. Only a short time ago brilliant excavations carried out in the region of Tehuacán have in great part lifted the veil from the mystery.

It was proven that about 5000 B.C. chili peppers, amaranth, avocado, and squash were already being cultivated. In the following millennium domestic corn—of which there are so many ancient and modern varieties—made its appearance. A short time later the bean and zapote were cultivated.

The plants mentioned, as well as other cultigens, would later form the basis of the native diet. The most widely utilized trio is that of corn, beans, and squash. But neither beans nor squash had the importance of corn, which was the very heart of the economy and diet of ancient Mexico. Because of this it was the divine plant of Toltec tradition, sung by poets as we see in these Nahuatl lines from the fifteenth century:

> I am the tender Corn Plant,
> From your mountains I come to see you,
> I your god.
> My life will be renewed:
> Primeval man grows strong;
> He who commands in war is born!

The ancient Mexican would have paraphrased the Napoleonic saying about the force behind war being "money, money, and always money," with "corn, corn, and always corn."

Agriculture has an importance that reaches not only into economic life but also into the totality of human culture. Work in the fields transforms man into a sedentary creature, and obliges him to establish himself in a more or less restricted area. This induces him to build his home

VALLEY OF MEXICO

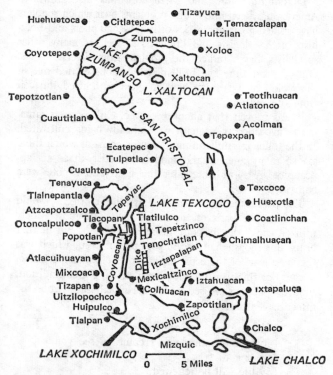

Fig. 2   The lakes, islands, and principal archaeological sites in the Valley of Mexico.

with increasingly strong materials in contrast to the huts of early times, which were surely no more than simple shelters of straw and branches. Upon learning how to till the land, man also creates the art of ceramics or pottery, an art impossible or difficult for nomads. This art was highly developed in America. Yet for the archaeologist its importance is even greater than for the ancient peoples, since it constitutes almost the only means he has for establishing the chronology of civilizations and the time sequence of different epochs and stages.

One of the great problems of the Mexican archaeologist is the almost complete absence of remains from the long millennia that separated the first American man from the period in which he began the ascent toward civilization. The hunters of big animals appeared and disappeared, the semi-nomadic bands gradually became at least part-time farmers—although they never stopped collecting and hunting—and then altogether sedentary. In spite of their cultural poverty, this was the time when many of the principal innovations originated that changed the American world and were the bases for the extraordinary development that we shall see later.

II. THE LONG CLIMB

The millennium and a half that ended shortly before the Christian era began marks, for the Valley of Mexico and the important areas surrounding it, the slow path leading to civilization. It was not a continuous upward climb but had sharp rises followed by moments of regression. In this chapter we shall point out the principal stages.

About 1500 B.C. the people in the Valley of Mexico were mostly farmers who lived in fixed villages, practiced the art of ceramics, and wove textiles; they also had various utensils of polished stone. In a word, paleolithic man had come to an end in the central valleys and we are now in the full neolithic period. In America, however, one must use these terms with caution since the evolution was quite different from that of the Mediterranean civilizations.

Several groups were living around the great lakes: in Zacatenco, El Arbolillo, Tlapacoya, Tlatilco, and other localities. All had a common culture, but each site showed differences which in the following centuries would be accentuated in those places that received influence from other parts of Mesoamerica.

The population density was surely low and increased very slowly. Because of an extremely high rate of child mortality, scarcely one third of the children reached the age of manhood. Even among adults, it is rare for us to find skeletons of men or women who are more than fifty years old. Later we shall see an important change in this regard, which will in part clarify a great many points.

Besides the basic food plants that we have already mentioned, the list of crops gradually increased in different areas in accordance with the various climates; *huauhtli, chia* (a type of sage), cacao, chili peppers, innumerable fruits and vegetables like the avocado, tomato, and chayote; tubers like the sweet potato; plants for flavoring like vanilla, and many aromatic herbs gradually came into common use. The main alcoholic drink was pulque, a fermented drink made from the juice of the century plant. According to some traditions, it was not produced until much later, at the beginning of the Toltec period. It may have been much earlier, however. Pulque is still today considered the national beverage of central Mexico, although it is losing ground to German beer. Tobacco was used more as a medicinal plant than for the pleasure of smokers; this is indicated by the fact that pipes are not found in the Central Valleys until after the year 1000 of the Christian era.

Since a rather remote period certain maguey fibers were used, and a short time later cotton, to weave sumptuous, colorful materials, but unfortunately few examples have survived. Our knowledge of them comes from painted murals and the illustrations of hieroglyphic books.

Grain was ground on *metates* (milling stones), producing a flour that could be used to make tortillas. Later, dried vegetables were crushed in mortar bowls, as is still done today. The *metates* were of petrified lava with three short legs and a flange around the edge which allowed the grinding pestle to slide back and forth inside the rim. Afterward, flat *metates* appeared that were similar to present-day ones. With these a *mano* or cylindrical stone was used that extended beyond the edge of the grinding stone and made the work easier.

But to obtain the delicious tortillas that we still enjoy in towns and villages, one must cook the dough on a *comal* (a flat earthenware griddle), an ancient utensil that is still in use today. Uncooked herbs or the eternally roasted meat tends to become very tiring to one's taste. But happily in this period they began to make ceramics, which enabled them to cook and to season their food. With this began the rather complex gastronomic tradition of ancient Mexico. Although many of the dishes described in the chronicles would be highly exotic for Western palates, they still represent an advance in the culinary arts. The art did not, of course, reach its full development until after the period we are now examining. I am sorry not to have tried dishes of the Mexica (commonly but incorrectly called the Aztecs) as preserved in the recipes of Sahagún, for he claims that some of the food was delicious.

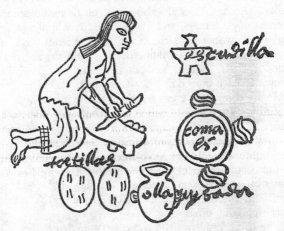

Fig. 3 Mexica tortilla-maker according to the Mendocino codex, plate 60. Drawing by A. Mendoza.
Escudilla = Bowl
Comal = Flat earthenware griddle for cooking tortillas
Tortillas = Round thin maize bread
Olla, gusado (guisado) = Pot for stew

Even the first ceramics, in simple forms and austerely decorated, show a technical perfection that implies a long evolution in the potter's art. This suggests that the knowledge of ceramic production arrived at the Valley of Mexico from other regions where antecedents have been found that date from about 2300 B.C., like those at Tehuacán (Purrón phase) or those from Puerto Marqués near Acapulco. In deep layers at this latter site appeared crude, almost unpolished vessels, although sometimes with traces of red color, that resemble those from Tehuacán. Perhaps the pottery found in these excavations is the most ancient of Mesoamerica and the beginning of a tradition that would become exceedingly rich.

The diet of the first inhabitants of Mexico was supplemented by gathering, fishing, and hunting. Animals were still relatively abundant at that time and there were deer, bears, boars, pumas, rodents, and numerous birds in the valley. The natives could also count on domestic animals such as dogs, turkeys, and ducks. The list is quite modest and it is obvious that the peoples of America were not especially interested in domesticating animals, as in the Middle East. Indeed, no other American animals are known to have been domesticated by man, except in Peru.

As the population grew, hunting became increasingly unrewarding. In the sixteenth century only the leaders ate meat. In the famous "Reports" sent to Philip II of Spain in reply to a questionnaire which he had circulated in all his empire, his subjects complained about this constantly.

From animal bones they manufactured utensils or jewelry such as necklaces, bracelets, earrings, and pendants. The hard stones—very scarce at that time in the valley—were surely imported.

The tribes lived in little rustic settlements consisting of scattered huts. These primitive houses were rectangular and built of adobe, or else the walls were made with the wattle and daub system that is still used today in native villages. It consists of covering a framework of sticks and branches with mud which when dry turns into a rather strong kind of mortar. This can be painted or whitewashed. What a violent contrast to the future cities made of stone, within a rigid urbanism!

Among the small items produced the most interesting are certainly the little clay figurines that have been found in great quantities and that almost always represent women. The *raison d'être* of these statuettes is still unknown. It may have to do with amulets used during fertility rites, for it is common to find them scattered in the fields. They may also have been a kind of household god similar to those used in Rome and preserved in the thatched huts, being at times buried with the dead. In any case these figurines did not represent well-defined gods with fixed attributes, as would be true in a later period. One can say that the gods were not yet born.

The figurines from this period and the following one are small, almost always solid, and modeled by hand. Facial

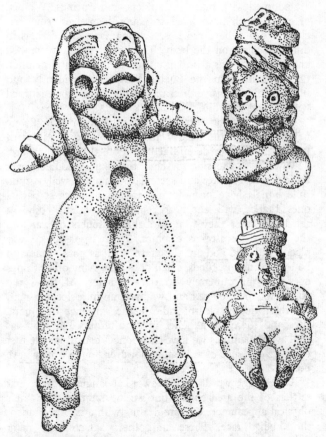

Fig. 4 Archaic statuettes almost without bodies. The head is joined to the limbs. Drawings by E. Abdalá.

features are indicated by means of rather broad incisions, or by adding tiny fragments, "pellets," onto the clay nucleus that forms the body and head, in order to depict the eyes, nose, mouth, or any other elements that protrude. The figures are almost always nude. Some, for example, wear only a necklace; others, more modest, have a loincloth or a short skirt. At times the more coquettish female figures are adorned with bracelets, anklets, and earrings. Women of every epoch have liked to paint themselves: some archaic figurines have red lips, a yellow face, and designs in different colors on the body. The hair is carefully combed and frequently has a turban on top in the oriental manner. One woman from the Puebla Valley was evidently outfitted by an expensive dressmaker: she wears a hat adorned with flowers and birds.

In the Valley of Mexico tombs, properly speaking, were never built and the dead were simply placed in pits with no set direction or determined position; they face upward, downward, to the side, or have their knees doubled over their chests. Primary and secondary burials as well as multiple burials have been found, and in some cases partial ones, that is, with the head separated from the body. In the latter cases they were probably prisoners of war and the heads were used as trophies. A variety of objects was placed with the body in the grave, such as pots, stone and bone implements, foods, small dogs, and many other things of which unfortunately no trace remains. At times the corpse was painted red and wrapped up in a sleeping mat. All these details clearly indicate the existence of funeral rites and therefore a belief in an afterlife. This cult, as well as the figurines we have mentioned, constitute the first concrete evidence of a religion, however simple it may have been.

Regrettably, we do not know what language these first settlers of the area spoke, but we are familiar with their physical appearance. We are dealing with a narrow-headed, short-bodied race. These and other characteristics mark them as being unquestionably the direct ancestors of the Indians of later periods.

It is difficult to imagine what the family, social, and political organization of these groups may have been. Nevertheless, their life was probably similar to that of other groups who at a comparable stage of cultural evolution lived on until the historical era. They give us a general idea which may with caution be used to draw parallels with our peoples.

The early inhabitants were gathered in small villages with an organization as yet very democratic, for there is no indication of class differences. We can distinguish only the beginnings of a division of labor. Apart from this division of labor by sex, which was a natural phenomenon, their highly perfected pottery, for example, leads us to assume the existence of skilled artisans, of potters. This does not mean that all their time may have been devoted to such work, but it does show that pots were not produced by every member of the community, but rather by a few who had mastered the craft. It is also possible to suppose, making analogies with later cultures, that we are dealing with truly professional potters, with people who devoted themselves exclusively to this art, who went from town to town producing in each place the quantity of items that might be "placed in the market," moving then to the next town in periodic cycles. This also suggests that the buyers had an excess production of their own goods to barter for pieces of manufactured pottery. Such a system still exists in Guatemala but quite possibly it began in a later period than the one which concerns us here.

The arms they used seem to have been made for hunting rather than for war. One must not forget, however, the possible presence of war prisoners in some of the graves.

The kind of life I have tried to describe was found to a greater or lesser extent not only among the inhabitants of the Mexican Valley, but also in other groups settled everywhere by that time from the mouth of the Pánuco River in the north to El Salvador in Central America.

They were peoples with similar cultures who, established in this vast region, constituted the first permanent population known there. They were, therefore, the basis of all later civilization. This fact is of supreme importance: it demonstrates that from such early times a part of the Americas was inhabited by human groups who were bearers of a basically similar culture. Within the same geographical borders this situation continued throughout the long pre-Columbian history. Naturally the boundaries of this region were not altogether permanent, but a single civilization lived within this area for at least three thousand years. We see here a group of peoples who lived side by side—variations were only local or temporal—who shared a common basis and a parallel history. They form, therefore, a his-

Fig. 5   Figurine from the Valley of Puebla dating from the end of the Formative Period. Drawing by E. Abdalá.

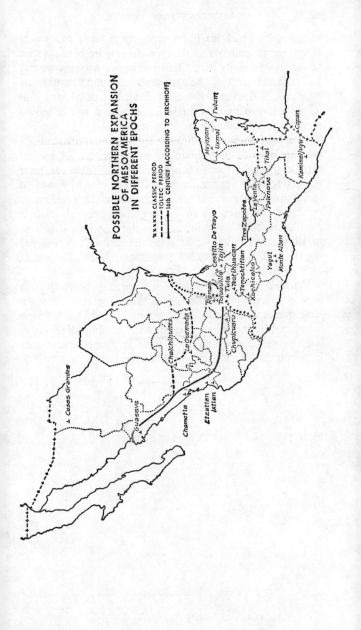

POSSIBLE NORTHERN EXPANSION
OF MESOAMERICA
IN DIFFERENT EPOCHS

xxxxx CLASSIC PERIOD
- - - TOLTEC PERIOD
——— 16th CENTURY (ACCORDING TO KIRCHHOFF)

torical unity which it will be necessary to study as a whole if we are to understand its evolution or even the occurrences in one of its parts. This section of America we call Mesoamerica. In this book we shall focus our attention on only one of the parts, the Central Valleys of Mexico. But in order to explain this particular section, it will be necessary to refer frequently to other areas.

As always happens with all peoples, the primitive stages are the longest. Only gradually is the rhythm of human invention accelerated. In this case too the life and customs do not seem to change. After a colossal effort by men to transform their existence from a nomadic to a sedentary one, and from hunters to farmers, they plunged for half a millennium into a period of calm during which it is hard to distinguish any specific steps forward. They enjoyed the fruits of their victory but they also sank into the morass of traditional custom.

Without a stimulus, the heart scarcely beats. It was only a millennium before Christ that they awoke from a long dream and began to move rapidly, driven by new forces and by formerly non-existent needs. Imitating Toynbee, we might say that they arose to climb a new step in the long, thorny path toward civilization.

III. THE OLMECS APPEAR

After the centuries of inactivity that we spoke of, a powerful influence began about 1000 B.C. in the Central Valleys, coming directly or indirectly from the first civilization of ancient Mexico that had evolved on the Gulf Coast.

This exerted a vital influence, and the great style it produced was characteristic of the art and much of the development in this period and those that followed. We find it, for example, in Gualupita and other places in the state of Morelos, but its classical site in the Valley of Mexico was Tlatilco. Explorations there have produced a fantastic collection of figures, pots, and other artifacts in an extraordinary style that is related closely to the great Olmec civilization.

The region where this blossomed is a vast alluvial plain and hill area furrowed by great rivers between the Papaloápan and the Grijalva. With a very high temperature most of the year, the land is extremely fertile, but in the rainy season it is subject to frequent flooding. The most characteristic and developed sites of the Olmec world are La Venta, Tres Zapotes, and San Lorenzo.

The Olmecs were not great architects and their buildings are only of secondary interest. This may be due to the almost total lack of stone in the region. On the other hand, there was already in La Venta an urban planning that presaged the future Teotihuacán. We also consider the Olmecs among the most extraordinary sculptors that Mesoamerica ever produced. We can say that they were the inventors of sculpture and their monuments represent the first appearance of this art. Some of its characteristics are monumental heads and stone altars; enormous statues by people who loved the grotesque; jaguarlike mouths and massive lips. The stone for carving these great works of art was brought from far away, sixty miles as the crow flies. Probably dragged to the beach, it was then transported by sea and by rivers on great rafts. All this, as well as the culture in general, points to a social organization far enough advanced to achieve such feats despite a primitive technology.

The human figure is portrayed in a peculiar form that is unique to this culture: generally nude but with no indication of sex; at times wearing a simply adorned loincloth; short, fat bodies with feminine traits that suggest the eunuch; short legs and deformed heads in the shape of a pear or avocado. The heads are of two quite different types. The more common one has a snub nose and thick lips, fat cheeks with bloated and slanting eyes, a jutting chin, and a mouth with deep furrows at the sides. This type represents a man with jaguarlike features, or rather it unites human with feline traits in order to form the extraordinary combination of a man with the face of a child and a jaguar—the god of the Olmecs. The second type is rather Armenian, with a fine aquiline nose and delicate lips. In other traits it resembles the preceding style.

These two anthropomorphic types are found in the great stone monuments and in the splendid bluish jade figurines so precious to these people, as well as in hatchets and other objects in which the jaguar and man are combined. As with the archaic peoples of the valley, the Olmecs modeled women in clay; and these belong to a still earlier stage of the culture in which there were no gods wearing special adornments and clothing, but only man in stone and jade. If we consider that the first gods of the Central Highlands were also masculine, we see that Mesoamerican religion began with attention directed to gods and not goddesses, in contrast to popular magic that depicted women in clay. Since we find gods of both sexes in this period—as we shall find until the end of pre-Columbian Mexico—it seems as if there coexisted a magic in which feminine figurines were venerated and an early religion in which male gods were the object of worship. Goddesses appear only later in the

jaguar was ⚹ to Olmec

Valley of Mexico and we shall not find them among the Olmecs.

This artistic people used jade in many other ways. They made beads of it, breastplates, emblems, pendants, polished gems, masks, ceremonial axes, and a great number of different objects whose use we do not know, like the beautiful jade boat with incised hieroglyphs, and an alligator formed from a chain of rings. As Miguel Covarrubias said, Olmec art "is in the spirit of the early cultures: simplicity and sensual realism of form, vigorous and original conceptions. The 'Olmec' artists were mainly concerned with the representation of a peculiar type of human being made up of solid, ample masses . . . They delighted in the smooth, highly polished surfaces of their jades, broken occasionally by fine incised lines to indicate such supplementary elements as tattooing, details of dress, ornaments, and glyphs. These lines are sharp and precise, soft curves and angular shapes with rounded corners . . ."

The sensational honor of inventing the Maya calendar probably belongs to the Olmecs, and it is among them that we find the two oldest legible dates in the American world. One is engraved on a little jade figure that depicts a duck-billed man—another association of animal-man so typical throughout Mesoamerica—called the Tuxtla Statuette and records the year A.D. 162. But the earliest date, now complete, is on Stele C of Tres Zapotes and indicates the day 7.16.6.16.18 of the Maya Long Count, equivalent to September 2, 31 B.C.

The correlation with the Christian calendar known as Correlation B is used here since it is the more probable one, although certain data suggest that we cannot altogether reject the one called Correlation A. According to it all the Maya dates would fall 260 years earlier than those of Correlation B. The Tuxtla Statuette would thus indicate the year 97 B.C. and the stele from Tres Zapotes March 2, 290 B.C.

As centuries later the cultures of Nahuatl origin took the eagle as their symbol, so the Olmecs devoted all their fervor—or terror—to the jaguar. This appears everywhere, as an animal or as a semi-person in the figures we have already described. The concept of associating man with an animal seems to be basic to Mesoamerican thought. It is an intimate association, we might say a necessary one. It portrays the *nahual*, the magic belief that a person's life is linked by destiny to an animal which is the *nahual* of that person. But the animal itself is deified in part, for it is also the *nahual* of a god or rather the god also has his *nahual* by which he is represented. So we have among the Olmecs the jaguar-man or the duck-man or more exactly the jaguar-god or the duck-god. In Teotihuacán the bird-serpent-god flourished, that is Quetzalcoatl, or the serpent-god Tlaloc, god of rain. Later, the various Tezcatlipocas were an eagle-god and the sun itself.

Recent investigations suggest that the Olmecs already worshiped several deities, the same ones that we will find almost three thousand years later in the Mexica period.

So among the Olmecs—and we could give many more examples—we find developed or in rudimentary form a great part of the amazing advances of the Classic period: intense ceremonialism, great sculpture, organization into social classes directed by priests, technical skill in working hard stone, significant astronomical knowledge, and above all the symbol itself of civilization: writing.

In the Valley of Mexico, Tlatilco is the bearer of that style which we have seen culminate in Veracruz-Tabasco. We must consider Tlatilco, however, as only a reflection of the principal Olmec sites, for we find there no architecture, great sculpture, or calendar glyphs. The part of Tlatilco excavated is a cemetery in which many burials were found, accompanied by vessels, figurines, and other objects. The male skeletons have certain feminine traits which is interesting in the light of the aforementioned depiction of men who look like eunuchs. As we have noted, this is characteristic of Olmec art. A considerable longevity has been observed for women. Another phenomenon is that of frequently deformed skulls and mutilated teeth. It is probable that they performed trepanations to relieve brain disease, but with disastrous results for the patients.

For later times we have proof of cases where patients withstood the operation and were cured.

The ceramic ware at Tlatilco is highly developed with a wealth of pots, vases, and elegant pieces admirably made and decorated. At times they depict realistic animals or ones stylized with great beauty. Among the figurines are some so similar to those produced at La Venta that they might easily be confused. They show an aesthetic ideal of big heads, short arms, tiny waists, and bulbous legs with extremely broad hips. One old text shows us that more than two millennia later the same preference for this latter trait was evident. The *Toltec-Chichimec History* states in speaking of Huemac, the last king of Tula, who began his reign as a child:

"When he was a young man, Huemac ordered his house to be guarded by Nonoalcas. The Nonoalcas thereupon told him: 'Rest assured, my prince, we shall do as you desire.' Thereafter the Nonoalcas attended to the house of Huemac. Then he asked for women and said to the Nonoalcas: 'Furnish me a woman. I command that she be four palms wide in the hips.'

"And then they brought him a woman four palms wide, but he was not yet satisfied. 'She is still not wide enough,' he said to the Nonoalcas, 'she is not as broad as I would like! Her hips barely measure four palms. I want them wider.'"

But let us leave Huemac and his exotic tastes to note that in Tlatilco the women heightened their elegance by dyeing their hair red; others combed their hair in braids or let it hang down their back. Their wardrobe was ever increasing. Although some were ingenuously naked, others wore ballerina skirts or wide short pants decorated with hanging trims, or a simple loincloth. They also wore embroidered boleros, headdresses in a thousand different styles, or turbans.

Jewelry increased in variety and value. From their treasure chests the people of Tlatilco could bring out not only ornaments of bone or baked clay but also jade beads and earrings of fine stone. They had necklaces, bracelets, and

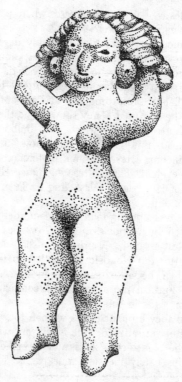

Fig. 7   Woman of Tlatilco. Drawing by A. Mendoza.

anklets. They also painted their faces and bodies yellow, red, blue. Those who were not afraid of the pain had their bodies tattooed to become more beautiful.

Certain figurines perhaps represent magicians, a kind of shaman with a sinister profile. Their faces are sometimes masked, suggesting other aspects of religious life. We are not yet dealing with true priests but with a combination of the magician and the healer.

There are a series of masks, too, some of extraordinary beauty. The most notable represents life and death: one side of the face has flesh, the other is a bare skull. Some are of animals, probably symbolizing the totem of the one who wore them. In certain excavations, figurines with two heads and a single body have come to light. Perhaps these were an attempt to illustrate in primitive form the basic principle of all pre-Columbian civilizations in Mexico: the cosmic and creative duality, the masculine and feminine elements joined in a kind of hermaphroditism, the good and evil which have the same source.

Tlatilco represents a step ahead, a less rustic quality within the culture of the valley, an evident contribution of new blood. But this is not the only site in the Central Highlands or the region surrounding the Valley of Mexico where the Olmec presence is felt. From Tlapacoya (Ayotla) come ceramics that are very typical of the Olmec world, not only in form and paste but in their decoration and in the figurines that accompany them.

We have already mentioned other areas where the Olmecs may have established colonies. Sites in the Valley of Puebla and in the Toluca region are notable, but it is in Morelos and Guerrero that many Olmec traces survived—not only portable objects but monuments as well. The sensational petroglyphs of Chalcatzingo leave no room for doubt about the type of people who carved them and in what period. The paintings in the Justlahuaca and Oxtotitlan caves in Guerrero are also partially Olmec. Besides, they are the oldest ones we have found.

IV. THE VALLEY MOVES TOWARD CIVILIZATION

In spite of the Olmec presence in the valley and the beautiful objects it left, the Central Highlands remained a peripheral region and we find little of importance there from those centuries when great achievements were being made on the coasts of Veracruz and Tabasco as well as other places of Mesoamerica. When the outside influence ended in about the eighth century B.C., the valley towns seem to have been left in a still quite primitive stage.

El Arbolillo, Zacatenco, Tlapacoya, Tlatilco, Chimalhuacan, and other sites that had been established in more ancient times continued to thrive. Many new ones appeared, such as Ticoman and Cuanalan, and while they never became more than villages or small towns with less than two thousand inhabitants, they had a role in the considerable increase of the valley's population. Excavations at Ticoman show that man now had a longer life span than before. This is evident from the number of men and women who died at an advanced age. The greater density presented new problems and also augured important developments and changes. Most of these had their roots in previous forms rather than in traits brought from somewhere else.

A new influence came into the picture, much less powerful than the Olmec one. Though not yet clear, it reveals elements that perhaps originated in West Mexico. Its importance is minor and the culture it represents disappeared rather quickly from the Central Valleys, although it survived a long time in its country of origin.

Houses of this period were mainly of adobe—as yet without shape but well utilized—and no differentiation is seen between them. This suggests a still uniform society without social classes, which we believe evolved only later in this region. Our information also indicates the existence of a series of small, more or less independent political entities that do not yet combine into large units with broad territories and dependence on a central power. At Ticoman the first recognizable god appeared, a head of the fire god Huehueteotl, which means "old god," a name that could not be more appropriate. This Nahuatl word—much more recent than the god itself—is perhaps the translation of an ancient name.

We have already spoken about the considerable demographic increase that occurred at that time. This would be inexplicable—and the advances soon to take place even more so—without the beginnings of a new political and religious organization and a more stable economic basis.

Let us begin with this latter aspect. Because of atmospheric conditions a period of increasing drought gradually overtook the whole region, causing a lower water level in the lakes. This new situation had extremely important repercussions for the inhabitants of the valley. Under the primitive conditions that existed, agriculture became much more difficult; the flora changed appreciably and the number of wild animals decreased; it was no longer so easy to obtain food. Once again it was the lakes and springs that decided the fate of the valley population. If man wished to survive, he had to revise his methods of production or create new techniques that would bring him sufficient crops from the dry soil.

During this period the first signs of new agricultural techniques may have appeared, quite modest at first: the beginnings of irrigation. It is possible that toward the end of the period a network of irrigation canals carried water from small rivers to the lands, thereby improving the system. The great aqueducts did not appear until later, when it was necessary to supply the cities with drinking water.

The famous *chinampas*, still visible today in Xochimilco and elsewhere, were perhaps started on a limited scale several centuries before Christ, but their great development took place in the Mexica period. With this procedure it was possible to use lake shores for agriculture by raising the ever fertile mud from the lake bottoms. Now that we have dried up the lakes, the last traces of this ancient form of agriculture are about to disappear.

Another well-known means of increasing the arable land is to build terraces on hillsides. We still see these on the slopes of mountainous Mesoamerica, although of course most of them do not date back to such remote periods. The increase in population forced some communities to establish themselves not along lake shores but in the piedmont areas. Here the ecological conditions and crops that could be grown were somewhat different, and therefore certain groups had better land than others. Perhaps this was one of the causes for the social differentiation that was increasingly apparent.

This state of affairs must have had important repercussions on all aspects of human life, as always occurs with an economic revolution. For example, irrigation is not usually the result of one man's efforts, but of the collaboration of a whole tribe or even of several towns. To accomplish and maintain such an enterprise man must renounce part of his freedom for the collective good; and for the project to succeed, the group must be organized and led. Work has to be planned and executed collectively. The tribe, therefore, must follow orders of a single leader or of an especially qualified group. This tends to create an elite class distinct from the rest of the society; while on the one hand this is the basis of social progress, on the other it tempts the leaders to organize the new society to their own advantage. Once the elite is established it becomes hereditary and forms the ruling class. The leaders of ancient Mexico were originally magicians; at the very moment they ceased to be shamans and turned into professional men of religion, they became priests. If a society is built up around a religious group, the whole civilization will normally be oriented toward a mystical concept, which forms the core and reason of its being. And so we see the birth of ceremonialism, which left its mark on the native civilization.

Apparently it was in Cuicuilco, in the southern end of the Valley of Mexico, that the first great monuments were erected. The oldest one was perhaps an oval-shaped foundation made entirely of earth. Later on the so-called Pyramid of Cuicuilco was built, which is really a truncated cone eighty feet high made of four tiers connected by a ramp and stairway. Uncut stones were simply placed one on top of the other, without cementing mortar. In its first phase the building was smaller and had only two tiers; the others were added later. As we see it today, only a general resemblance to the original form remains, for it has not been possible to reconstruct it exactly. On top of the mound a square thatched-roof altar formed the temple itself, of which few vestiges are left. Around the central building were other temples of smaller dimensions, making it the first of those ceremonial complexes that we shall find later in all the monumental cities.

This incipient ceremonialism, indicated by the presence of temples and the appearance of the first concrete gods, is reflected as well in the new burial methods. The dead were still frequently placed in very simple tombs, but the walls were now covered with stone and roofed with flagstones. Bodies were buried in rather precise positions and not by chance as in the preceding period. Offerings to the dead gained in importance.

All these momentous changes—perhaps the major ones of Mesoamerican history—directly initiated the climb toward civilization. The beginning is already apparent at Cuicuilco, with its ceremonial architecture and residential site for the elite. Cuicuilco occupied perhaps thirty hectares and was the most outstanding center—which we can already consider almost urban—of the southern end of the valley. But pyramids were also built at Tlapacoya and the rich tombs excavated there indicate a relatively advanced social stratification.

Meanwhile, in the northeastern section of the valley a series of towns began to develop at an ever increasing pace; these later would unite in the great city we call Teotihuacán. This did not yet exist even in fantasy, but the region's exceptional location, in control of the only permanent springs able to irrigate the wide alluvial plain, gave it increasing importance. This was not the only reason—nor the principal one—but we do know that the two main towns of this period, later to form part of the city itself, had approximately five thousand inhabitants and occupied about four hundred hectares.

Under these conditions it was natural to assume that the hegemony of the valley would be divided between the two main centers and that the tradition of allegiance to local political bosses (caciques), while limited to those two of previous times, would continue. But the gods ordained otherwise. It was not water but fire and volcanoes caused by an eruption from little Xitle over Cuicuilco that changed the picture. A thick layer of lava covered not only the monuments of Cuicuilco, but also a vast region south and west of the Valley of Mexico—that region known today by the name of Pedregal (stony ground). Where the first temples of the Central Highlands had been erected, on those fields of petrified lava, University City has been built in our days.

The disaster of Cuicuilco was to benefit the site that later became Teotihuacán. With the disappearance of its rival power, Teotihuacán's population rose, although probably not due to migrations from Cuicuilco. The period we call Teotihuacán I started at this time. About two centuries before the Christian era, building began on one of the most remarkable structures of Mesoamerica: the Pyramid of the Sun. Except for that of Cholula, erected many centuries later, the Pyramid of the Sun is the largest monument ever constructed in ancient Mexico. It contains nearly a million cubic meters and rises more than sixty meters high, an enormous mass of adobe held up by stones, without a single adornment. Ornamentation would first appear in the following period on a structure annexed to the pyramid.

On top rose a temple of which only the foundations remain today. At the time of the Spanish Conquest an enormous monolithic statue stood over the altar of the vanished temple, but for religious reasons this statue was smashed to pieces in the sixteenth century.

The colossal pyramid, poorly restored during excavations at the beginning of this century, does not present today the aspect it must once have had, and its circumference has been greatly reduced. But in the seasons from 1962 to 1964 the structure built onto the front was correctly restored, partially recapturing the form it had, not in the period we deal with here but in the following one.

The first Pyramid of the Moon also belongs to Period I and apparently at this time the general outline of the city was at least laid down, that is its north-south axis—badly named the Street of the Dead—and the transversal axis that we call the East and West avenues. Teotihuacán probably covered at that time an area of sixteen square kilometers and had roughly thirty thousand inhabitants.

The gigantic nudity and the learned geometry of these pyramids and of the urban planning are wholly directed toward the grandiose and the sublime. Their sheer size makes us realize how great was the power of the religious elite who could undertake and erect a monument of such enormous proportions. They must have had available both technicians and a multitude of workmen, as well as extensive financial means to enable them to feed the army of men building the temple, which was unable to produce its own sustenance.

V. THE GOLDEN PERIOD

To the first centuries after Christ belongs that era of ancient Mexican history which we generally call the classic period. It represents the highest point in the evolution of the civilization of Mesoamerica. The length of this period varies according to regions, so that, for example, in the Valley of Oaxaca, it probably extended to the end of the eighth century and even later. The same seems to occur in the Petén region in Guatemala where the Mayan culture flowered. The last stele of Uaxactún was erected May 4,889, according to Correlation B. Two other cities, of less importance, Xultún and Xamantún, show the same date and a jade plaque was inscribed in the year 909. With these final dates the prodigious system of the Mayan calendar, which might be considered as a symbol of classical society, disappeared forever.

In the Central Valleys this period seems to have been shorter and ended perhaps about the middle of the seventh century. It was marked above all by the high development and the disappearance of the city of Teotihuacán.

Around the great pyramids of the Sun and the Moon (Plate 7), reflecting the preceding culture, a new city was built, developed, and later died, the greatest city in ancient Mexico. For the first time we can use the word city rather than town or village, since in Teotihuacán we are not dealing with a somewhat rural culture, but with a fully urban civilization.

The problem of the "cities" of Mesoamerica has been widely argued. It is clear that in most cases we cannot think of cities in our sense of the word, for they consisted of centers where during market days the inhabitants from a rather wide circle of surrounding hamlets came together, and considered this place as their center of activity. The center had actually very few inhabitants although it possessed a swollen number of temples and public monuments in which priests and governors lived. This seems to have been the general pattern of Mayan "cities." On the other hand, Teotihuacán, as later Tenochtitlán, were cities of our kind, for apart from having a "downtown area" they also had a permanent large population. They were no longer religious meccas or markets which operated only once a week, but places with a dense population, with a bureaucracy, and distinct social classes that lived in different districts and also in houses of varying importance. A rural population that supplied the food was scattered around the outskirts of the city, living in innumerable villages and towns.

The population density in Teotihuacán—apart from the temples or public buildings—must have been substantial. At its zenith it had over 200,000 inhabitants and occupied more than 32 square kilometers. The fantastic quantity of accumulated constructions, ruins, objects, in a word, all signs of human life, suggests a population cluster on a scale hitherto unknown in Mesoamerica.

We have no knowledge of the Teotihuacán language, and next to nothing of their physical appearance, since they had the bad habit—bad for us grave-searchers—of burning their dead. Perhaps for this reason it has been impossible to find a single Teotihuacán grave which belongs to this period. We have uncovered many burials, however, either nearby or buried a few centuries later when the old capital had become a mere provincial village.

The ceremonial center was traced out and built along a longitudinal axis which was the great main street. It is called today Micaotli, the Street of the Dead. The name is surely of Nahuatl origin and the later baptism has no historical value.

At the far north end of the great street rises the Pyramid of the Moon in the middle of a magnificent plaza surrounded by temples and homes. Other temples and palaces border the street which is dominated by the mass of the Sun pyramid. At the other end—after crossing a river —is the so-called Citadel, in the middle of which rises the temple of Quetzalcoatl (Plate 8). Magnificent stone sculptures decorate the façade, portraying the famous plumed serpent, the symbol of this god. These heads alternate with masks of other divinities.

Some time later, another pyramid with much simpler lines was built on top of this monument, a real triumph of ritualistic architecture. Surrounding the entire structure is a low, broad wall almost four hundred meters long, which seems to connect the platforms and temples harmoniously in a rigorous framework typical of Teotihuacán symmetry. This whole complex and the great plaza opposite that perhaps served as a market seem to form the civic and commercial center in contrast to the northern section that was devoted to religion. The East and West Avenues lead into this immense quadrangle, thus dividing the whole city into four sectors. It is interesting to note that this would be precisely the plan followed later for Tenochtitlán. It is apparent that in this aggregate, as well as in every part of the city dedicated to religious purposes, a beauty based on grand, austere lines was sought, uninterrupted by curves or ornaments. This balance of forms put the monuments in harmony both with each other and with the stage of the surrounding mountains. There seems to be an aesthetic relation between these mountains and the contour of the city, which gives them both a quality of eternity (Plate 9).

In the central zone there were only temples and palaces reserved for the rulers and priests. But further out were the residential suburbs. Ruined houses appear on all sides, and among some which have been explored we note the existence of several kinds of houses. The most luxurious ones contain a quadrangular patio with surrounding rooms, or a grouping of several patios and rooms to form a palace, a real apartment house. In Teotihuacán for the first time we find an architectural style which continues almost without change until the end of the Indian period. It consists of a talus and vertical wall adorned with a panel; the steps always have flanking balustrades. The walls are covered with a coat of very fine white stucco, frequently painted with frescoes. Fortunately a great number of these paintings, at least fragments of them, have been preserved, and

Fig. 8 Figure from the frescoes of Tetitla, Teotihuacán. Drawings by A. Villagra.

they are virtual books which allow us to probe into the religion, customs, and life of the ancient inhabitants. The principal themes of these paintings are religious, but one can notice at least two different styles.

The first and most common is that which we shall call the "official style." Especially, gods or priests are portrayed in splendid attire. The clothes and accompanying objects indicate one divinity or another. We find a vast accumulation of masks, green feathers, embroidered ceremonial garments, jewelry, etc. The attributes which surround these divinities recall the powers of the central figures. So, for example, Tlaloc, the god of the rain, is framed with motifs which emphasize the importance of water, the basis of all agriculture and one of the themes which constantly obsessed the Indian. We also see leaves and water flowers, and hieroglyphs which unfortunately we cannot yet read.

In the second style, though also religiously inspired, gods no longer appear: we find men who render homage to the gods or else the dead who enjoy the delights of paradise. It is this latter group which allows us to reconstruct the clothing, jewelry, objects, games, and even certain attitudes and expressions. In one fresco the theme is the paradise of the rain god Tlaloc, where the drowned go as well as those who have died from diseases magically related to water. The anonymous artist painted what men considered perfection on the earth. We see figures who sing, dance, or bathe in a river, others who play; the scene is a dense orchard of trees and beautiful flowers or delicious fruits, and also butterflies, birds, and fish (Plates 10a and 10b).

It seems to me that the paramount interest of this painting is that it reveals to us what was the ideal or desideratum in life of an extinct people; this is a rare find for an archaeologist. In depicting a paradisiacal place, the Teotihuacán artist shows us what he considers to be the perfect life, the place of every pleasure, the location where everything highly esteemed in real life appears in abundance. Man usually thinks of heaven as the place where he is to fulfill his terrestrial desires, where the things he knows suddenly become easy and perfect. So this painting shows us something of the philosophy and aspirations, necessarily based on concrete reality, of the Teotihuacán people.

Both earth and vegetable colors are employed in the painting. The most frequently used hues are dark red, vermilion, and various tones that go from green to turquoise blue, and yellows.

Indian painting, from the Teotihuacán period until the end, never ventured into chiaroscuro. Figures are flat and always without shading. Perspective is arrived at only by placing more distant persons or objects on a higher plane; there is no effort to reduce size as they move back from the spectator. The size of figures is in relation to their importance and not in relation to distance. So the gods appear larger than men.

We do not have many examples of Teotihuacán sculpture, but the few we have reveal an excellent technique and a monumental conception, even when dealing with small objects. Undoubtedly the most important statue which has been preserved is that of a goddess, perhaps a goddess of the water, on exhibition today in Mexico's National Museum of Anthropology (Plate 11). It is an admirable example of Teotihuacán aesthetics, which at-

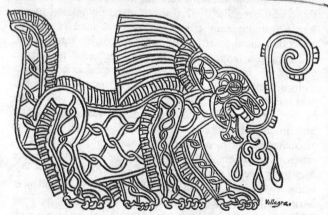

Fig. 9   Tiger in a suit of mail. Teotihuacán. Drawing by A. Villagra.

tempts to simplify everything, which transposes reality into geometry and preserves essential elements, suppressing all details. Afterwards, a less austere style appears in the sculptures on the temple of Quetzalcoatl, in the magnificent marble vase depicting a tiger, found today in the British Museum, or else in the merlons that complete the façades of houses and which we still find later in the Mixtec codices or in Tenochtitlán.

The production of clay figurines is as important as in the preceding periods, but the technique is entirely different; it is no longer done by hand, but in a mold. The gods have been industrialized. These same molds, found and utilized by today's inhabitants, permit them to sell tourists an inexhaustible production of statuettes which are only half false.

In contrast to the archaic statuettes, which were always anonymous, the Teotihuacán ones were increasingly precise in identifying concrete gods. Thanks to these sculptures and paintings we have a list of Teotihuacán divinities. With the exception of the Tezcatlipoca gods, who only became important again in the Toltec period or later on, all the gods are represented in Teotihuacán, including some that were lost with the disappearance of the city.

We also have small portraits of heads notable for their naturalism and the simple beauty of their traits: wide forehead, fine nose, lightly protruding cheekbones, and admirably drawn mouths. They are one of the examples of Indian plastic art closest to our own aesthetic.

In addition to so much progress in architecture, sculpture, and painting, Teotihuacán produced an enormous quantity of different objects: ceramics of varying forms and techniques, jade or stone jewels, and, in short, a thousand things which a dense, refined population manufactures when it lives several centuries in the same place. Teotihuacán is also the first great producer of stone masks in ancient Mexico, although not the initiators of this idea, which was continued later among the Toltecs and the Mexica. The Teotihuacán masks do not, evidently, represent an individual person or a god: they always reproduce the same triangular, sharp-angled face with highly delicate features, serene and rigid. They were made of various kinds of hard stones. They were surely not masks for the living, but were placed on the dead to protect and shelter them from sorcery. The cheekbones or a transversal band were at times inlaid with jade mosaic.

It is surprising what a small number of hieroglyphic inscriptions we find in Teotihuacán, especially in comparison with the exuberance of Mayan inscriptions from the same period or the rather substantial number from the Valley

Fig. 10   Heads of Teotihuacán statuettes. Drawing by E. Abdalá.

of Oaxaca. Of course the custom of erecting stone steles is not characteristic of the Central Valleys since their presence there is always exceptional.

Long caravans moved from one end to the other of Mesoamerica to exchange products with those of the tropical regions. In this way the influence of the great city of the high plain was disseminated all the way to Central America. Teotihuacán exported ceramic ware and diverse objects, which we have found in the tombs of Monte Albán, in Oaxaca, at Kaminaljuyu in the Highlands of Guatemala, and at Tikal in the Petén.

Its influence spread into Veracruz, western Mexico, and even over the barbarians in the north. All this indicates an era of peace and prosperity, of commercial transactions and interchange of ideas between different peoples; it all suggests great development. Mesoamerica spread out at the expense of the nomads, and in that northern area they built cities along the rim of the cultural orbit extending out from Teotihuacán. Possibly these same cities were the focal points from which the future invaders left. Teotihuacán, in her eagerness to expand, created those who would put scorpions to her breast and destroy her.

Another happening of this period is the differentiation between the cultural areas of Mesoamerica. During the archaic period and even in part of the formative, the styles had much in common with each other and clear differences were not yet apparent. From now on we distinguish at least the Mayan world from the non-Mayan, which we call, anachronistically, the Mexican sphere. This does not mean that there was no common basis between these two worlds; the common ties began in the remote archaic period and were sustained by intercommunication due perhaps to trade. It does signify, however, that now certain clear characteristics of one area do not pass over to another. So in Teotihuacán we do not have the steles, nor the corbeled vault, nor the zero of Mayan mathematics. Curiously, a ball court has never been found there either.

Teotihuacán is a typical example of a great open city which did not have the intention of defending itself. Finding itself the head of an empire it must have reasoned, there were no enemies who could think of attacking it. The serenity of this capital was truly imperial. The gods planted or brought rain but there are few representations of armed warriors. Religion was master of the city but this should not lead us to assume that it was a true theocracy, a system of government that would seem to preclude an empire. Rather it is the first example, which—as in so many other things—its successors would copy, of a dual system in which civil or military leaders and priests rule together, however much the former apparently are subordinate to the latter.

The urban pattern that the Toltecs and Mexica would imitate had been established. Teotihuacán had fixed forever in Mexican history the preeminence of the valley, and our capital being established here is due precisely to the success achieved more than two thousand years ago by those Teotihuacán people whose name we do not know.

Their triumph was complete—insofar as humanly possible—and their urban world so complex that it is absurd to try to explain it on simple ecological bases or on the more or less doubtful importance of its irrigation system. It seems more credible that its early growth was due in part to ecological and hydraulic factors, in part to its control of certain prime materials such as obsidian, in part to its unique position straddling the valleys of Mexico and Puebla—perhaps because of this the Avenue of the Dead extends five kilometers farther to block the passageway—and especially to the real urban revolution achieved by Teotihuacán, which began a new type of society with a new political organization. It was also due in part to the preeminence it acquired as a great religious center. Upon all these solid bases the city developed more and more and its prestige grew by the day.

At its apogee it was a vast urban center with intense commercial activity, importing and exporting numerous products both near and afar. Religion itself became an economic force—in addition to political and cultural—since it attracted numerous pilgrims who came to render homage to the gods who permitted such grandeur. Thus it was a tourist center. As already mentioned, its position enabled it to dominate the two great valleys of the Central Highlands, which neither the Toltecs nor the Mexica were able to do later, whence their weakness. Only the Spanish Colony united these areas once again and it was not by accident that Puebla was the second city of the Viceroyalty.

Teotihuacán also became an "international" city—later characteristic of Mesoamerica—where people came from other areas to live and several languages were spoken. We have certain proof of a colony from the Valley of Oaxaca and indications of others from the Totonaca and Huasteca regions.

But as the centuries passed, the distinguished ruling class, as is bound to happen, became a dominating minority which oppressed rather than guided, and so the signs of decadence appeared. Toward the seventh century the city lost its creative power and began to fall apart internally. Its prestige diminished; then, as in Rome at the end of the Empire, it became an easy prey for all those nomads who for many years had wished to take possession of the city. One of the more daring groups must have overrun the old capital, sacked and burned it. The traces of the fire are still visible in the carbonized beams which dirtied the whiteness of the stucco and in their fall tore down the splendid painted murals.

Today, after a thousand years of abandonment and pillage, the sacred city is still magnificent and imposing in the austerity of its wisely open spaces combined with the majesty of the pyramids. Here everything was done to elevate the soul of the onlooker. It was not a matter of pleasing but of exalting.

VI. THE INTERREGNUM

Although Teotihuacán left embers whose flames would rise again, with time the identity of the early inhabitants was obscured. Their history was transformed into a myth. The later immigrants in the valley were astonished by the dimensions of the structures and thought that they could only have been built by a race of giants: the Quinametzins of Toltec legend. And as a "scientific" proof of the veracity of those giants, what could be better than to find their bones? So the prehistoric animals whose remains are even today abundant in this region became the giants. The real mammoth confirmed the mythical Quinametzins. This legend was believed by the Spaniards in the period of the Conquest, and in order to convince Charles V they sent as proof the femur of an elephant. What a strange destiny for the bones of that ancient animal!

But the Teotihuacán ruins were to acquire a still greater magical importance. Confused by the large dimensions, the Toltecs thought that if giants had built the city then gods must have inhabited it. In fact the word Teotihuacán both to the Mexica and Toltecs meant "the place where the ancients lived" or "the place of the gods." For this reason legends have placed the creation of the Fifth Sun in Teotihuacán.

This idea of the Fifth Sun comes from the Indian way of conceiving history. While for Western man history is a more or less continual ascending line—a concept which curiously takes in both Christian and evolutionary ideas— for the Mexican Indians history was a series of closed circles. Each one, independent of the other, disappeared with a tremendous cataclysm in such a way that at the end of each era the gods were obliged to create everything anew, including the sun and men.

We know very little about the two or three centuries between the destruction of Teotihuacán and the beginning of the historical era, properly speaking, in the Valley of Mexico, which seems to divide again into several wards, each with allegiance to a *cacique* (local political boss). We can affirm only that it was a period of low culture during which many of the advances of the previous period were forgotten and in which the descendants of the Teotihuacáns were more and more mixed with the invaders. This slowly raised the cultural level of the barbarians, who gradually absorbed part of the old heritage.

This vacuum in the history of the Valley of Mexico does not correspond to events in other areas which were not destroyed by the invaders of Teotihuacán. So the Mayan centers in Petén continued erecting stone steles and buildings until the end of the ninth century. Precisely in this period the Zapotecs of Monte Albán were in a great period of building. It was actually then that this people became the great architects of ancient Mexico and strewed the valley with innumerable constructions. Even nearer, in Puebla Valley, the great pyramid of Cholula was erected.

But by the end of the ninth and the beginning of the tenth century, the crisis which destroyed Teotihuacán was dispersed through the entire Indian world. It caused the death of many, many great cities of the earlier periods. All the Mayan ceremonial centers of the "old empire" disappeared, as did Monte Albán, although in these cases there is no evidence of fire or that a conqueror pierced his spear through the roofs of the temples as shown in the hieroglyphs. It is clear that there must have been profound causes for this kind of collective suicide. Wars, plagues, droughts, earthquakes, breakdown in the agricultural system, etc., have been imagined to be the cause, but none of these explanations is convincing. One may imagine that an internal social disorganization slowly undermined their resources and weakened the peoples to the point where they disappeared or were ready prey for an outside conqueror. Indeed, the tenth century shows a great internal laxity, a suspension of activities due perhaps to a weakening of the vital motor impulse. Possibly, as in the specific case of Teotihuacán, the elite groups that carried these peoples to unsuspected heights had lost their creative force; and having become the sole dominating minorities, they were swept away by internal forces. The latter are represented either by the uprising of an oppressed class or by two groups in conflict—perhaps the military against the priests—or by a new religion which, coming from the masses, acquired the necessary force to overthrow the old gods.

We can be quite certain that at least after the eleventh century Tezcatlipoca, the god of the Toltecs and of all their successors, became the most important divinity. This change in emphasis is coupled with numerous transformations in the very concept of religion. While Quetzalcoatl was opposed to human sacrifices and to the brutal religion of conquest, Tezcatlipoca demanded them and, as we shall see later, this demand had transcendental consequences in the destiny of the Mexica. From the beginning of Toltec history a conflict arose between the two religions, a conflict which continued until the moment of the Spanish conquest, even when at that time the new religion had almost completely vanquished the ancient one. We must not, of course, exaggerate, in speaking of the two religions, since fundamentally they were the same. What does change is the importance given in one case or another to different gods and the consequences, sometimes enormous, of this diversity of cults.

The end of the classical world, however, did not always mean the end of all the cities which existed in that period. So some that flourished in that era continued afterwards. The most interesting example we know of in the Central Valleys is Xochicalco in the Morelos region. Its influence, although indirect, was very great, since from there, culturally speaking, came the historical Quetzalcoatl. In combination with other influences the remnants of the ancient religion seem to have been preserved, as indicated by the cult of the plumed serpent.

From a rather remote period there were inhabitants on the hill of Xochicalco, and in the classical period the most important building was erected that remains today. It consists of a small pyramid whose interest lies in the magnificent bas-reliefs that surround it and which constitute a mystery. Great plumed serpents comprise the principal elements in the decoration. They are located in the talus of the building, which is crowned with a jutting cornice of great elegance and adorned with sculpture. Between the bodies of the snakes are human figures, in a style that distantly recalls the Mayan, and also groups of hieroglyphs, whose deciphering is even today very dubious and has been the subject of numerous interpretations.

The fact that this central pyramid was dedicated to Quetzalcoatl, as the great plumed serpents indicate, allows us to conclude that Xochicalco was a place dedicated to this god. This is very important in regard to the inception of Toltec history, as we shall soon see.

One proof among others that Xochicalco did not disappear with the destruction of Teotihuacán, but rather prolonged its history to concur with that of Tula, is that their game of ball-court with rings is identical to that of the Toltec capital, and surely its contemporary; another proof is the frequent discovery of objects which chronologically and stylistically correspond to the finds in Tula.

Although built on a hill, Xochicalco was difficult to defend. The inhabitants during those turbulent times found it necessary to build a fortress on a nearby height. It is perhaps the oldest example we have in the Central Valleys of a city which lived with the fear of a possible attack. The fortress, contrary to what one might expect, did not intend to defend the city from invasion; it was rather a place where the inhabitants might take refuge in case of need and wait there, with relative security, for the withdrawal of the enemy troops.

In this city, as in others of the period, great rigorous

perspectives are no longer sought, in which the perfection of the straight line is the essential element, in which ornamentation is superfluous as at Monte Albán, the most admirable plaza in America. A more lavish ornamentation, a less refined line, a barbarous luxuriance, a greater movement, these are some of the characteristics of the new cities. The Xochicalco style is truly a transition style between the austerity of Teotihuacán and the more precious art of the Toltecs.

* * * *

Tajín is another link between the classical and the Toltec world.

There, amid the heat and the jungle, a people who were predecessors of the historic Totonacs erected that extraordinary, immense city which even today is so poorly known. The principal pyramid of Tajín, seven stories high, is one of the most impressive buildings of pre-Columbian art (Plate 12). The wall-panels of each floor are decorated on all sides with niches that give great movement to the building. It was believed, erroneously, that these niches contained gods or some other object; but in reality they are simply an architectural decoration. A great stairway, also decorated with niches, leads to the upper temple. This stairway presents an additional interest, for here the relationship between Tajín and Xochicalco is vividly clear. It combines certain characteristic elements of Mayan architecture, vaguely present in Xochicalco, with the typical stairway form of the Mexican pyramid.

The bearers of Tajín culture, perhaps the Pipiles, spread in many directions, especially at the end of the classical period. So we see them deposit their objects on the ruins of the Palace at Palenque, and it is possible that they were the destroyers of the marvelous Maya city, which disappeared at the end of the period. Its influence on Tula is not very notable, perhaps, because Tajín was already in its decline. It disappeared so completely and the jungle devoured it to such an extent that at the time of the Conquest no one was aware of its existence and we had to wait until the end of the eighteenth century for Padre Alzate to mention for the first time this gigantic ruin.

*   *   *   *

As we have noted, the year 900 marks the most important change in the history of ancient Mexico. The written documents that we possess do not go back before this date in the Valley of Mexico, and therefore they signal the difference between the historical and pre-historical age.

Outside the Central Valleys the situation is quite different. We have documents which reach back into much more ancient periods, some of which we have already mentioned, such as the stone inscriptions found in Olmec culture, among the Mayas or the people of Oaxaca.

The most celebrated of all, the Mayan steles, indicate dates which extend over a period of approximately six hundred years. In addition, we can read a series of calendar items such as the position of the moon at a given moment, the annual correction necessary to include the difference between complete days, and that true and bothersome solar course of 365 days and a fraction, which has caused so many complications and which neither Caesar nor Gregory XIII corrected perfectly in their systems of leap years.

But all this has not given a single datum of written history, perhaps because till now it has not been possible to decipher many of the hieroglyphs, though these steles probably show dates only in a religious sense, for the days themselves were like gods. Only occasionally do they contain some historical data that we so much wish to find.

The stone inscriptions at Monte Albán perhaps refer to conquests or other events. But here too our ignorance of their system of writing prevents us from affirming anything concretely.

Other documents which are much more important historically are the hieroglyphic books which come from the Mixteca. Whether by chance or because of some real fact, most of the books which survived the great shipwreck in which the high Indian culture sank during the sixteenth century derive from this region. Thanks to them and to the most brilliant work of Alfonso Caso, we have been able to establish dates for real events as of the beginning of the eighth century. Of course, the books do not relate to us a complete history, but, as with medieval chronicles, the dynastic and military history of a few men. For example, in Tilantongo, we know the list of their kings, with the dates of their birth; the names of their wives and their origins; their children; the wars and victories which they had; and the ceremonial accidents of their lives. But we know little of the peoples whom they governed or of the fundamental problems of their government.

To those data we must add other inscriptions that appear in mural paintings or in painted ceramics, and which because of their extensiveness, as in the case of the famous frescoes of Bonampak, suggest a store of historical data. We cannot read these either.

But up to the period that we are studying, only isolated hieroglyphs appear in the Valley of Mexico and probably without any historical meaning. On the other hand, the new peoples preserved a record of their adventures in real books—as those of Mixteca—in which generally legible hieroglyphs permit us to reconstruct at least the important outlines of their history. For this reason it is correct to consider that with these written documents the historical age began.

The ancient cultures of the Valley of Mexico had frequent contacts and were still strongly influenced by the established peoples on the Atlantic coast, the tiger worshipers. But the new groups which we shall study are a typical product of the plateau and their distinctive animal is the eagle. From this moment on, the eagle of the high valleys vanquishes the tiger of the tropical coasts.

If we wish to apply the terms used in the classification of European cultures—actually inapplicable to America—we can say that in this period the neolithic age ends and a new age begins, marked at its high point by the use of metals. But each age is a curious paradox, for the neolithic age marks the apogee of the Indian cultures and the age of metals brings almost nothing of real importance.

Metals were known and used in South America from
an earlier period, from Peru to Colombia, and their use
gradually extended to the north, across Central America.
During the Toltec period they began to be used in Mexico.
Nevertheless, metal never had a great importance in American cultures, and was much less important than in the
Mediterranean basin. Metals were for luxury rather than

Fig. 11   Small gold mask with bells. It is notable for its movable
jaw. It comes from the Chinantla. Drawing by A. Mendoza.

for their practical usefulness. Nevertheless, especially among the Tarascos, copper was abundantly used to make needles, pliers, awls, hatchets, and the cutting edges of farm tools. They also made jewels and ceremonial objects like the splendid copper mask preserved today in the Museum of Morelia.

The state and the Mexica lords had accumulated great supplies of metal, principally of gold, which have been completely lost. Today we read with intense regret the burning descriptions by Dürer or the chroniclers of the Conquest, or read of the list of wonderful objects sent to Charles V as a gift to the court. All was melted down in the crucible. The same must have happened to the jewelry found in searches, officially admitted, which were made in the sixteenth century, such as that of the Count of Osorno, President of the Council of the Indies.

This is why very few examples of Indian gold and silverwork were known until the splendid pieces were uncovered in the Sacred Cenote of Chichén Itzá and the sensational discovery of tomb 7 at Monte Albán (Plate 13a and 13b). There, in 1932, Caso found the grave of some Mixtec chiefs and a fabulous treasure—necklaces, bracelets, earrings, diadems, gold rings. Apart from their beauty, the jewelry reveals a technique, or rather, an array of very advanced metallurgical techniques such as fusing metals together according to the system of "lost wax" or "false filigree." In one extraordinary piece, half gold and half silver, we cannot see how the two metals were joined together.

Splendid pieces have also been uncovered, although less abundantly, in other Mixtec sites, in Guerrero, in the Huasteca and other areas of Mesoamerica. From there they spread to the Southwest of the United States.

This period of the interregnum represents a noticeable decline in Mesoamerican culture. Nevertheless, in addition to serving as a bridge between the classical and Toltec worlds and being the period in which metals were first known, the age was the beginning of the historical era.

VII. THE TOLTECS

The beginning of the tenth century is marked historically by the violent appearance of a semi-barbarous horde coming either from the Jalisco region or from the southern Zacatecas. It was the Toltecs who began a different world, a new world emerging from this period of disorganization. It combined the cultural heritage of the classical world with that brought in by the new peoples from the outside.

We know little about these peoples before their arrival in the Valley of Mexico. Their prehistory is rather mythical and may be reflected in their cosmological tales, as for example the Legend of the Suns. We have already mentioned the Fifth Sun. The four previous ones correspond vaguely to four former stages which may have some historical connotation. During the First Sun lived the giants, who were a crude people who did not "sow" and ate only pine kernels, like groups from the North of Mexico. They evidently represent a pre-agricultural stage of nomads. The Second Sun was when men were of usual dimensions and ate bread made with the fruit of the mesquite. With the Third Sun men knew how to sow but did not possess the divine corn. They ate a grain "which is born in water." The basic plant of the Fourth Sun is designated only by the esoteric name: "4 flower." The Fifth Sun represents new man, the peoples of the Nahuatl family who live in the historical or post-Teotihuacán era. They are now perfect men who possess, thanks to Quetzalcoatl, the perfect crop: corn.

The Toltecs came to the Central Valleys led by a great Chief, Mixcoatl, who must have had extraordinary qualities. His name and influence had repercussions in all the Indian chronicles. For the first time we can mention a specific man of flesh and bone. It is no longer a question of anonymous stories.

In a few years Mixcoatl conquered the Valley of Mexico and some neighboring regions, coming down like a whirlwind on the miserable remnants of the Teotihuacáns. Afterwards, Mixcoatl looked for a proper site to establish his capital. In Culhuacán he found a peninsula at the foot of the hill Cerro de la Estrella, full of caves, whose strategic location made defense easy. There the first capital was founded; and curiously this was also the only city to survive the great disaster which three centuries later was to annihilate the Mixcoatl empire.

Once established, Mixcoatl devoted himself to enlarging his conquests in several directions, and so we see him take over parts of Morelos, Toluca, and Teotlalpan.

During one of his campaigns in Morelos the chronicle tells us that he found himself before a young, beautiful woman who was not a Toltec:

"The woman Chimalman came out to meet him, she put her shield on the ground, and shot her arrows and darts; she remained standing, naked, without skirt or shirt. Seeing her he shot his arrows: the first one he shot only passed above her and she simply bent down; the second one he shot at her passed near her ribs and she simply bent the shaft; the third which he shot at her she simply seized with her hand; and the fourth which he shot at her, she caught between her legs. After having discharged four times, Mixcoatl turned around and went away. The woman immediately ran away to hide in the cavern of the great ravine. Again Mixcoatl came and readied himself with a supply of arrows; and again he went to look for her and saw no one. Immediately he began to mistreat the women of Cuernavaca. And he told the women of Cuernavaca, 'Let us seek her out.' They went to bring her and said to her, 'Mixcoatl is looking for you, because of you he is mistreating your younger sisters.'

". . . Once more Mixcoatl went there and again she came out to meet him; in the same way she stood revealing her completely naked body; in the same way she put

her shield and her arrows on the ground. Once more Mixcoatl shot at her and missed his mark. . . . After this happened, he took her, and lay with the woman who was
Chimalman, and she was then with child. . . ."

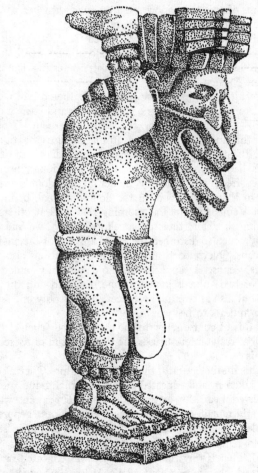

Fig. 12 The god Ehecatl, one of the appellations of Quetzalcoatl, in the form of an atlas. Drawing by A. Mendoza.

Actually, only after this event did the woman take the name of Chimalman, which means hand-shield, a name which she evidently deserved. A few months later, while Chimalman was pregnant, Mixcoatl was assassinated by one of his captains, who usurped the throne of Culhuacán. Because of this the widow sought refuge with her parents where she died on giving birth to a son.

This child, born in exile, was called Ce Acatl Topiltzin. Later he took the name of Quetzalcoatl, by which he is known in history. He was the most interesting figure in ancient Mexico.

Quetzal in Nahuatl is the beautiful feathered bird which is still found in the forests of Guatemala, and *coatl* means serpent—the bird-snake, or the plumed serpent. Esoterically, this means the precious thing or also the double thing, the twin. Among pre-Columbian Indians, the twin always had a magic meaning; it was feared and because of this, frequently killed. Whether in the double ear of corn, in the creative god, in the double animal, or in the planet Venus (at times a "morning star" and at others an "evening star," and therefore a celestial twin), we find this duality which so disturbed the mystical spirit of the ancient Mexicans. Quetzalcoatl in one of his appellations also represents Venus. He appears, therefore, not only under the form of two animals joined in one, the bird and the serpent, but also as two in one, since Venus is only one "star" which appears to be two.

All this of course refers to the ancient god Quetzalcoatl, but what really interests us is the man, the son of Mixcoatl, and his legend.

At his mother's death, the child—the future Quetzalcoatl —was taken in and educated by his maternal grandparents, who lived near the marvelous site of Tepoztlán, where there still remain traces of him in local folklore. Tepoztlán was akin to Xochicalco where, as we have already seen, the old religion was preserved and Quetzalcoatl was worshiped. That is why the young prince was educated in this belief, which was not his father's. With time, due to his brilliant qualities and the prestige of his birth, he became the high priest of the god Quetzalcoatl and took the name of the god in accordance with the native custom. This has led to constant confusion, since the god and the historical person have been frequently confused, the same as the numerous priests who in the course of centuries had the same title.

When Quetzalcoatl was a young man a legitimist party seems to have called on him to occupy his father's throne. But before returning to Culhuacán he sought out the remains of Mixcoatl and buried them in the hill Cerro de la Estrella. He built a temple on top and raised his father to the category of a god. Unfortunately, we have not had the luck to find the tomb which the faithful son dedicated to Mixcoatl.

The usurper was worried by these events and attacked Quetzalcoatl who, from the top of the hill, overcame him and killed him. With the death of the usurper who, as we remember, was also his father's assassin, Quetzalcoatl became the indisputable chief of the Toltecs. He attempted to give them the benefits of his maternal civilization and the cult of his eponymous god.

We do not know what his reason was for deciding almost immediately to shift his capital, but after a first attempt, which seems to have been unsuccessful, about the year 980 he settled definitively in Tula, which from that moment on became the Toltec capital.

Quetzalcoatl decided to construct a truly grandiose city and for this reason brought in artists and artisans from various places with a superior culture to that of the Toltecs, who in those days were scarcely beginning to assimilate the remnants of the old shattered civilization. In the nineteen years that he ruled, he built much and did it in such a way that a legend was created. With time not only all the structures of Tula were attributed to him but many others in which it is certain he had no part. So Sahagún describes the temple and home of Quetzalcoatl: "There was also a temple that was of the priest named Quetzalcoatl, much smoother and more precious than their homes; it had four rooms: one faced the East and was made of gold, and they called it the golden house because instead of being whitewashed it had sheets of gold and very subtly nailed together; and another room faced the West and it was called the room of emeralds and turquoises because inside, in place of whitewash, it had fine jewels of all kinds of stones, all set and joined together like a mosaic work, and this was greatly admired; and another faced the noon sun, which they call the South, and it was made of many mollusk shells, and in place of whitewash it had silver and shells that covered the walls and so subtly set that the joining was not noticeable; and the fourth room faced the North and this room was decorated with red stone and jasper and sea shells.

"Also there was another house with feather designs and inside it was covered with feathers instead of whitewash and it had four other rooms; one faced the East and this was of rich yellow feathers that replaced the whitewash and it was made of all kinds of very fine yellow feathers; and the room facing the West was called the room of plumage, and in place of whitewash it had all kinds of the richest plumes, the plumage from a bird that was fine blue, and it was very subtly placed on and adhered to blankets and nets which hung from the walls as a kind of tapestry, which they called *quetzalcalli*, which is a room with luxurious feathers; and the other room faced the South and they called it the house of the white feather, because inside it was all covered with white feathers in the form of tufts, and it had every kind of rich feather; and the other room that faced the North they called the room of red feathers and it was hung inside with all kinds of feathers from precious birds. Besides these houses they built many other very strange ones and of great value."

This rather fantastic description has a ceremonial interest and in it we can observe some of the ideas of the Indian mind: the ritual number *four* and the strict relation that existed between the cardinal points and certain colors: North and red; South and white; East and yellow; West and blue or green. These last two colors are interchangeable in Indian art; in fact, it is always one turquoise color and therefore a greenish blue.

As time went by, all the great things of the past were being attributed to Quetzalcoatl, who was depicted as a bearded white man. He was immensely learned and the inventor of all the good things from which man benefited. He gave man corn which he had robbed in the kingdom of the dead from the old god of the infernos. He was therefore the father of agriculture. He invented the ritual cal-

Fig. 13 Relief from the hill of "La Malinche" in Tula. It depicts Quetzalcoatl in the Toltec style, with his emblem Ce Acatl. Reconstruction by A. Villagra.

endar, and not only a way of measuring time but also the art of divining a person's good and bad luck according to his date of birth. The horoscopes, writings and books, medicine and all ceremonial ritual were his. We know perfectly well that this learning came from a much earlier time, but the attributions, though false, show us the absolutely unequaled prestige which this man reached before posterity and throughout his entire people. His century became the golden age.

"And moreover they say that he was very rich and had everything necessary to eat and drink, and the corn (under his reign) was in abundance, and the squash very fat, an arm's length around, and the ears of corn were so tall that they were carried with both arms and the canes of wild amaranth were large and fat, and one climbed them as one would a tree; and they sowed and reaped cotton in all colors, red and incarnate and yellow and brown and whitish, green and blue and blackish and gray and orange and tawny, and these colors of the cotton were natural and they grew from seedlings that way, and it is said that in the same town of Tula many kinds of birds were raised with rich and differently colored feathers, and other birds which sang sweetly and softly. And more than that, the said Quetzalcoatl had all the wealth in the world, gold and silver and green stones and other precious things and a great abundance of cocao trees in different colors, and the said vassals of the said Quetzalcoatl were very rich and lacked nothing, nor were they hungry nor did they lack corn, nor did they eat the small ears but rather they used them like firewood to heat up their baths."

We have already noted that Quetzalcoatl, besides being king of the Toltecs, was the high priest of his namesake god. This, naturally, led him to wish to impose the religion of his god upon the true religions of the inhabitants of Tula, that is, the cult of Tezcatlipoca. The ancient cult of Quetzalcoatl, unfortunately poorly known, is much more agreeable and more lofty in tone. It contains an element of monotheism: "They worshiped one lord alone whom they held to be god . . ." Some four hundred years later we shall see another great king expound the same superior religion, with the same lack of success.

Quetzalcoatl was opposed to the practice of human sacrifices: "He used to tell them often that he wanted only snakes and butterflies to be offered and given in sacrifice."

But this golden age, whose principal victims were the

[I] Plan of Tenochtitlán based on the map attributed to Cortez and published for the first time in the famous collection of Ramusio, Vol. 3, 1556.

[II] Partial view of the Pyramid of Cuicuilco.

III A] (*above*) Objects from Cuicuilco, showing the stratographical layer under the lava where they were found. [B] (*at right*) Huehueteotl head, Ticomán. (Vaillant, 1931, Plate LXXIX).

[IV A] (above) One of the colossal heads, La Venta. [B] (left) Dwarf in blue jade. Hill of Las Mesas.

[V] The famous statuette of Tuxtla.

[VI A] (*top*) Stele C, from Tres Zapotes. [B] (*above*) Mask from Tlatilco: the left side represents a live person, the right a dead one. Collection of Miguel Covarrubias. [C] (*left*) Statuette from Tlatilco. Collection of Diego Rivera.

[VII] Teotihuacán. Pyramid of the Sun.

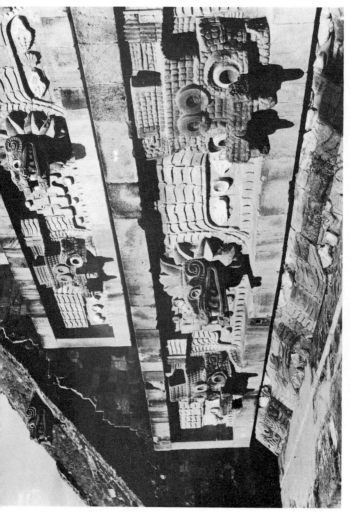

XVIII. Temple of Quetzalcoatl in Teotihuacán. Detail

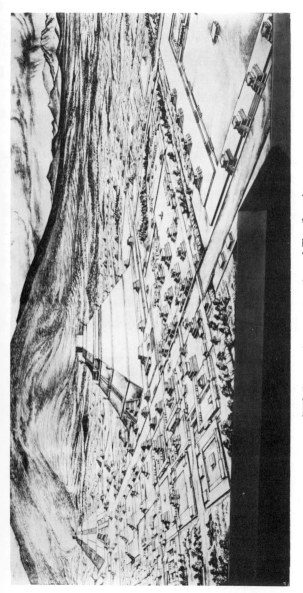

[IX] Panoramic reconstruction of Teotihuacán.

[X A] (*above*) The "Tlalo-can" of Tepantila. Detail.
[B] (*left*) Detail of above plate.

[XI] The colossal statue of the "Goddess of the Water," Teotihuacán.

[XII] The pyramid of the Niches in Tajín.

[XIII A] (left) Gold jewelry. Tomb 7 in Monte Albán. The upper part shows ball court scene. [B] (below) Mask of Xipe. Tomb 7 in Monte Albán.

[XIV A] (*above*) The Great Pyramid of Tula and the adjoining colonnade. (Photograph by J. Acosta.) [B] (*below*) The Atlantes and other columns in the upper part of the Great Pyramid of Tula. (Photograph by J. Acosta.)

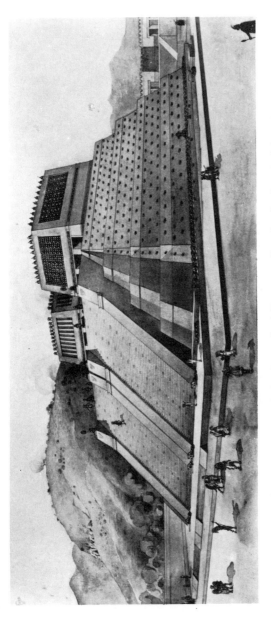

[XV] Reconstruction of the Pyramid of Tenayuca. Drawing by Ignacio Marquina.

LXVII. Reconstruction of the main square of Tenochtitlán with the Great Temple at the left.

butterflies, could not last and Quetzalcoatl, like the great religious reformers, had to end up as a victim of his faith. Behind the brilliant façade of Quetzalcoatl's Tula lived several different tribes, and they had not embraced this religion; rather, they still worshiped the bloodthirsty and terrible Tezcatlipoca. Their priests continually wove plots against Quetzalcoatl and his ultimate fall is attributed to acts of magic perpetrated by his rival, Tezcatlipoca. One day, for example, the latter appeared disguised as an old man in the house of Quetzalcoatl and asked his attendants to let him enter. They refused. But upon the insistence of the visitor, Quetzalcoatl was notified and he said: "Come inside, I have been waiting for you for many days." After Tezcatlipoca entered, he showed the king a mirror in which the latter saw himself and so "he gave him his body," which meant that on seeing himself for the first time in the mirror, he knew himself. Continuing, Quetzalcoatl informed the old man that he was very sick and that he had pains all over. The old man took out a medicine and after much insistence, succeeded in persuading the king to drink it. It happens that the medicine was *pulque*, the inebriating drink of ancient Mexico. Once Quetzalcoatl drank the first glass, he asked the old man for more and ended up by getting drunk. This was inadmissible in a high priest. But the worst was that during his drunkenness he had a priestess brought in and he slept with her. With this he lost the purity which was an indispensable requisite for a priest.

This legend, and many other similar ones, shows us how his enemies tried to topple Quetzalcoatl, not so much in his capacity as king as in his position as a religious representative. Indeed, what we sense in this episode of the last phase of Quetzalcoatl is the struggle between two religious groups, or more probably between a priestly group and a military group which wore the mask of the Tezcatlipoca priests.

At the moment that Quetzalcoatl lost his prestige as a representative of his god, he found himself obliged to abdicate as king, for in his case both aspects were indissolubly united. This does not mean that the curious duality of rule which we shall perceive later did not exist in Tula.

In the year 999 Quetzalcoatl left Tula. During his life, followed by a certain number of the faithful, he traveled through the Central Valleys. Among other signs of his having been there were arrows with which he pierced trees, leaving them thereby transformed into crosses. He settled for a short while in Cholula and later made for the coast, where he set sail for Yucatán, the black and red land. Before his final departure Quetzalcoatl promised to return someday, from the East, to recapture the throne which was rightfully his and to reign in peace over his subjects. Remembering that legends describe him to us as a bearded white man, and recalling the crosses on the trees and his final promise, we understand why, five hundred years later when Cortez came ashore in Veracruz, Moctezuma II was quickly convinced that he was dealing with Quetzalcoatl who was returning to reclaim his legitimate rights. Under these conditions, struggle was useless since one can not vanquish a god.

To this we must add that by an extraordinary coincidence, Cortez disembarked precisely in the year 1 Acatl, which was the year that Quetzalcoatl had promised to return.

Traditions say that the Toltecs, led by Quetzalcoatl, arrived in Yucatán and after conquering the local inhabitants settled in the Peninsula, mainly in the area called Chichén Itzá. Undoubtedly this is a legendary simplification of facts which could not have occurred exactly in this way. Probably, a Toltec group first settled in some place along the Gulf coast, where they remained in contact with the Mayas sufficiently long to impose themselves upon them and to learn their language imperfectly. The conquered people referred to the Toltecs as "those who speak poorly," that is, people who use Maya as foreigners.

Later they undertook a new migration which was to lead them to the conquest of Chichén Itzá. It was a small but strongly knit group, composed of chiefs and priests who managed to overcome the Mayas. The result of this conquest was the new city of Chichén Itzá, where the Mayan architectural elements were combined, and surely very felicitously, with elements brought in by the Toltecs. We have several buildings which give proof of this artistic union. The most important ones are the Temple of the Warriors and the Castle. In both sites pyramids were constructed in the central-Mexican style; snake columns were erected, head downward and tail forming the lintel; columns of warriors were built and many other typically Toltec elements appear there. Only the roofs of some temples built according to the system of false vaults, which is exclusively Mayan, and the ornamentation suggest that we are dealing with Mayan workers directed by Toltec architects. The situation is similar to that of the first Spanish-Mexican churches in which the missionaries directed the work and imposed their European style; but the workers who did the actual work were Indians and left a sign of their labor in innumerable details conceived and executed not in the European manner but in accordance with the canons of Indian art.

But all this does not explain the similarity between Tula and Chichén. It is too close, there are too many identical things, even in the measures and details for it to have been due to a memory which the Toltecs of the ancient plateau capital had taken with them. It seems almost as if the same architects had supervised the constructions in both cities, only in Chichén they added Mayan ideas which they found on the spot.

The god of this new Maya-Toltec Chichén Itzá is the same Quetzalcoatl but his name was translated into Maya as Kukulcán, which means exactly the same thing, that is, the plumed serpent.

As time went by a nationalistic Mayan reaction set in, slowly at first and with great force later on. The Toltec elements and influences disappeared until the day arrived when the conquest was forgotten, and the elements brought in from the center of Mexico faded from the peninsula. So the posthumous importance of the two great Toltec capitals was totally distinct, for while Tula, though destroyed, continued to have a strong influence on the new peoples who inhabited the region, the Toltec predominance in Chichén Itzá disappeared altogether.

In fact, the great Mayan culture never developed again and the last centuries marked a continual decadence until the peninsula, divided up into many small states, became an easy prey for the conquering Spaniards. The Mayan civilization disappeared from the scene of history without fire or blood, without falling as did Tenochtitlán wrapped in flames of glory.

* * * *

The kings who followed Quetzalcoatl in Tula were of slight distinction. Even now the list raises unresolved chronological problems. Only a few legends survive as part of the history. So, an Indian chronicler tells us that one of these kings, Tecpancaltzin, one day received a very beautiful young girl who came with her parents to bring him a gift. This consisted of the honey of the maguey, that is pulque, which the king received with great pleasure, and he was even more pleased with the girl who brought it. He asked the parents to send him this gift again and for their daughter to bring it. When the girl returned the king filled her arms with gifts and "was very happy and treated her as if he had been fond of her for many days, begging her to meet with his desires and he gave his word to do many good deeds to her parents and to her as well. Thereupon, they paused a good while over these requests and answers, until the girl, seeing there was nothing else she could do, agreed to carry out what the king ordered. And having fulfilled his desires he had her taken to a place a little bit outside the city and surrounded with guards and sent word to her parents that he had procured certain ladies to undertake her education, because he wished to marry her with the neighboring king in return for the gift which she had brought him, and that they should not be troubled, that they should consider her as being in their house, and thereupon he granted them many favors and gave them certain towns and vassals so that they were lords of them and of their descendants. And her parents, although they were very much grieved, disguised their sorrow, for as it is said, where there is force right is lost." This is one of the few stories with a human feeling that we know of from the series of the lords of Tula. This legend, as the one about Quetzalcoatl's drunkenness, suggests that pulque was invented only in this period.

During these reigns evolved the artistic complexity which archaeology has called the Toltec style.

Although the Toltecs inherited many elements from more ancient cultures, they produced an art in which many new things were invented and which acquired a great character. As in almost all the art of Mesoamerica we see it appear in its fully developed form. Apart from some vague antecedents in western Mexico, its origins remain concealed in the shadows of history. Nevertheless, it clearly represents the collision and fusion of the new people, the Nahuas with the remaining inheritors of the ancient civilizations.

The great pyramid at Tula (Plate 14a) dedicated to one of the appellations of Quetzalcoatl, who is represented as a "morning star," is a magnificent example of the new style. It extolled not so much the gods or priests as the glory of military triumphs. Entering the wide vestibule of the fifty-one square columns, the priest could admire the long, multicolored procession of warriors sculptured in single file along the walk (Plate 14b) which was finished off with a jutting edge decorated with green snakes. As he walked by, he perhaps poked the fire of the incense burners and mounted the steep stairway. Before him he saw one by one the five sections of the pyramid with their brilliant bas-reliefs: grotesque masks of human faces emerging from the gullet of a serpent decorated with bird feathers; hieroglyphs of eagles eating hearts or drinking blood; processions of jaguars and pumas tamely wearing a collar and bells. Above, in the center of the stairway, one came across a sculpture of a reclining god—Chac-mol—who held a tray with the purpose, perhaps, of receiving offerings; this figure was reproduced in innumerable examples not only in the

Central Valleys but in far Yucatán. In front was the sanctuary, whose roof was topped with merlons in the form of snails, and held up by two great columns of serpents with open gullets resting on the floor, their tails pointing upward. As the priest went through the columns he would encounter a row of four immense atlantes portraying silent warriors with arms in hand, the great butterfly breastplate on their chests, a crown of turquoise and feathers, and kilts held up from behind with a big round ornament. Their faces, like all those from Tula, are completely devoid of expression; they look square and solemn. They have nothing of the eternal beauty of Teotihuacán and also lack the vigor of the Mexica sculptures. Beyond was the temple itself, enclosed by four square columns with bas-reliefs on each side, also representing warriors on two of them and bunches of arrows on the others; one motif separated from the other by the very stylized faces of the earth monster painted in lively colors. Finally, at the very back one would find the altar: a great monolithic table held up by atlantes in plumed dress and many rows of necklaces. There the offerings and sacrifices were placed. But unfortunately, we know nothing of the statue of the god itself, if indeed there was one.

At the other side of the pyramid is the coatepantli, a small area surrounded by a wall decorated with interlocking serpents with skulls, and marked by two rows of Greek frets. Above, the white merlons finish off the building. These coatepantlis—one of many innovations—were reproduced in all later temples and in much greater size in Tenayuca and in Tenochtitlán.

On a holiday afternoon the warriors could take part in the game of ball, which was already an ancient sport. But the Toltecs had added one more difficulty. While before it was perhaps only a matter of getting the ball into a goal on the other side of the field without touching it with their hands or legs, now they had to pass it through a stone hoop so narrow that it could hardly get through. The ball was made of rubber and although the game had a religious symbolism, it allowed the rival teams to bet high stakes and at times even their own person, so that if they lost they had to give themselves up as slaves to the victor.

With the passage of time the Toltec people, still so barbarous under Mixcoatl, had become the chief representative of native culture, which together with the ever vivid prestige of Quetzalcoatl made the later inhabitants consider the Toltecs as the great civilizing people.

Their fame was so widespread that according to the chronicles, "They were the great architects and carpenters and were skilled in other arts such as silversmithing; they produced gold and silver and cast them together and cut precious stones and made the best things in the world, and were, in turn, necromancers, spell-casters, witches, astrologers, poets, philosophers, and orators, and were proficient in all those arts; the good arts as well as the bad; they had corn, cotton, chile, frijoles, and the other grains that grow on the earth; and they were the best painters in the earth and the women were excellent spinners and weavers; they wove very elegant robes of a thousand colors and figures, which they loved and which were as fine as those of Castile; and they wove blankets in many ways—some seem to be of velvet and others of fine cloth; others like damask and satin; others like delicate linen and others like coarse linen; as they wished to and had need to." "Their buildings were of stonemasonry and hewn stones and *tesontli,* they used stone troughs and water gutters for drainage as do our Spaniards; they had baths to bathe in and many other things which would be very long to recount."

The last king of Tula, Huemac, which means "great hand," ruled about seventy years. Initially, his reign was very happy but with time came a series of calamities. First, there were tremendous droughts and hunger, and afterwards invasions of nomads brought about probably by the drought. To this can be added an internal crisis which was due perhaps to the fact that the Toltecs, having reached the summit of their power, concentrated their efforts on extracting tributes from the conquered peoples payable in luxury items such as feathers or precious stones, and they forgot the economic needs and especially the growing of corn.

Since its settlement the population of the city of Tula was mixed, and included several distinct groups in a constant state of effervescence. Each of these groups had a god, foreign to the Toltecs and frequently inimical. Under the reign of Huemac, the Toltecs, desperate upon seeing that their own god did not listen to them, took their prayers and sacrifices to the gods brought in from outside. These gods acquired considerable prestige, and under their protection the importance of foreign groups in Tula increased. The unceasing rivalry aggravated the internal crisis.

These historical events are also related to us in legendary form. We are told that one of the enemy groups in Tula sent one of their demi-gods named Tohueyo, disguised as a modest seller of chile. The young warrior, naked as was the custom of his tribe, sat in the market to sell his poor merchandise. The market was situated in front of the royal palace, where King Huemac's only daughter lived, who was beautiful and who had been courted unsuccessfully by all the Toltec chiefs.

"And the said daughter of Lord Huemac looked toward the marketplace and saw Tohueyo naked, and his genital organ, and after having seen it went back into the palace and took a sudden fanciful desire for the organ of the young Tohueyo and then became very sick because of the love for that which she had seen; all her body was swollen and Lord Huemac learned that she was very ill and asked the women who guarded his daughter: 'What illness does my daughter have?' And the women replied to him: 'Lord, the cause of this sickness was the Indian Tohueyo and she is sick with love for him.' The king ordered his men to search for the seller of chile who had disappeared. At last they found him and brought him before the king. The latter ordered him to cure his daughter. Tohueyo refused. But the servants took him, washed him, painted his body, dressed him sumptuously, and brought him to the bedroom of the young girl who 'then was cured and regained her health.' And in this way Tohueyo became the son-in-law of Lord Huemac."

This family tie so annoyed the Toltecs that the majority of them, offended by the preponderant place given the foreigner Tohueyo, rebelled against Huemac. In the legend, Tohueyo evidently represented magically the diverse foreign peoples and principally the Huastec groups who had settled in Tula and whose ever-growing influence forced the Toltecs to attack them.

A series of revolutions broke out which ultimately forced Huemac, in 1168, to flee from his capital. He took refuge in Chapultepec where he seems to have committed suicide years later, around 1174. With him the Toltec empire disappeared. But the material fall of the metropolis and its final ruin in 1224 were only a consequence of these internal convulsions. Weakened by revolutions, abandoned by Huemac, situated as it was at the frontier of the civilized world, it fell into the avid hands of the northern pillagers.

This position near the frontier, probably chosen by Quetzalcoatl when Tula could defend itself against any invader, became another cause of weakness toward the end of its history.

Nevertheless, although Tula may have lost its political importance, it still preserved an unparalleled prestige. We see how even after the conquest, the Moctezumas were to use the title "Counts of Moctezuma of Tula." On the other hand, its art served as a basis for those who followed, to such an extent, that the Mexica, in full power, tried to carry off—perhaps to Tenochtitlán—the great Toltec sculptures. They did not succeed in their attempt and left them strewn at the foot of the demolished monument.

But the greatest importance of Tula in the destiny of Mexico seems to be that there the socio-political pattern was established which continued to the end. Tula inaugurated those militarist empires, brief and flashing, whose ultimate representative was the Mexica state.

VIII. THE NEW BARBARIANS

With the fall of Tula another great wave of nomadic peoples came like a tornado into the south, invading the lands of sedentary peoples, uprooting all in their wake. They were the barbarian hunters who once more confronted the civilized farmers. With Tula conquered, there was no power strong enough to oppose their incursions. We know these nomads by their generic name of Chichimecs. This word does not mean a specific tribe, but rather an aggregate of groups, at times very different, who were allied at certain moments and at others fought among themselves, and whose common trait was their semi-nomadism. The word Chichimec in Nahuatl probably means, "lineage of dogs." We should not give this name the infamous meaning that it would have for us, for it most probably referred to a tribal name in which the dog was the totem of the tribe; we find this frequently in several other parts of America, and even today at times in central and northeastern Mexico. After some time the meaning of this word was enlarged to include not only the original Chichimecs but all the recent arrivals or those emigrants who led a nomadic life. Therefore, in a general sense, the word came to signify the opposition between the barbarian Chichimec and the civilized Toltec. It is also possible, as Jiménez Moreno has suggested, that the name Chichimec comes from an old legend of Huichol origin. It is said that the mother of the gods spoke to a woodcutter announcing to him a flood in which all men would die. To be saved he would have to enclose himself in a hollow tree trunk in the strange company of a bitch. The woodcutter did this and as the goddess closed the tree trunk very tightly, it floated until the flood waters receded and the woodcutter and his bitch came out. They settled in a cave and he made a daily outing to cut wood. As the woodsman was the only surviving man he was most amazed upon returning to his cave each day to find jars of river water and hot tortillas. Overcome by curiosity, he decided to hide and then he saw the bitch shed her skin and turn into a woman. While she went to the river to bring water the woodcutter burned the dogskin. The woman immediately began to scream, feeling terrible pains in her shoulder and indeed her shoulders were burned the same as the dogskin. The woodcutter threw the water on her with which she was kneading the dough for the tortillas, and so she was relieved. Afterwards they married and their children acquired the name "lineage of dogs." Perhaps because of the memory of this story, when the Chichimecs first appeared in the Puebla Valley the inhabitants threw the water of *nixtamal* on them and called them sons of dogs.

At first glance it is somewhat difficult to understand how those nomadic hunters could gather sufficient force to lay siege to and even conquer the established empires. But the ruins of Chalchihuites and especially La Quemada, as well as places in Durango, Querétaro and elsewhere indicate that these tribes, although fundamentally nomadic, were not all so. They had built centers where they probably gathered for holidays or for trading, and these served as a nucleus for the scattered groups. During centuries they received Teotihuacán and Toltec influences and many civilized traits. La Quemada, in Zacatecas, was a city of considerable extension surrounded by many other villages which depended on it as a permanent source for provisions. This source could only be agricultural; that is, here as elsewhere, small agricultural islands were formed, with some power and wealth, in the area of the nomads. In other words the frontier of Mesoamerica extended farther north than in the sixteenth century. These sites demonstrate the existence of groups with a more or less permanent unity and a population rather larger than that which a simple tribe of hunter-gatherers could ever have had. Nevertheless,

La Quemada, with all its size and the evident power it represented, was far from attaining the refinements of other cities of the period. The buildings were made of unhewn stone, without mortar. The walls were not covered with stucco and we do not find any trace of murals or sculpture. This is true in all the settlements in the north of Mesoamerica.

It is probable that the numberless hordes set out from this or from other similar cities when at different moments

Fig. 14   The island of Aztlán. Drawing by A. Villagra.

they began their assault and conquest of their neighbors
to the south.

Among these groups, one of them was of minimum importance and probably took part only as a spectator, or
at most had an insignificant role in the toppling of the
Toltec empire. In time it was to stand out in an extraordinary way. We are referring to the Mexica, who appear for
the first time on the scene of history.

The oldest data which we have about them are semi-
historical or semi-legendary. It is recounted that they came
out of a cave situated on an island called Aztlán from
which the name of Aztec is certainly derived, although
"Mexica" is more correct and hence the Mexican of today.
As time passed and their grandeur increased they adopted
the name of Culhuas to indicate their Toltec or civilized
ancestry.

They were, at the time, a small tribe led by four
chieftain-priests whose only possession was a bundle in
which a statue of a god was wrapped, unknown until that
time: Huitzilopochtli. Upon his tribe's triumph, this god
became the great god of the Anáhuac. After lengthy immi-

Villagra.

Fig. 15 The porters of Huitzilopochtli during their peregrina-
tion. The first one carries the god's bundle on his back. Sigüenza
codex. Drawing by A. Villagra.

grations they settled in the area around Tula, and there took place a mythologico-astronomical event which was to weigh heavily upon their future destinies. The legend narrates that an old widow was living in Tula, whose behavior was beyond reproach, who had had a daughter and four hundred (that is to say innumerable) sons. One day this pious lady was sweeping the temple when she found a ball of feathers which she concealed between her breasts. A few months later she noted that she was pregnant and a little later her daughter and her sons became aware of it. Outraged by what they considered to be their mother's levity, they decided to kill her. The "four hundred" sons armed themselves and marched on the widow. At this moment she heard a voice within her saying to her: "Do not be frightened"; and a great and vigorous son was born armed from head to toe, like the classical Minerva. He carried in his hands an *atlatl* and a sword, and also a new divine weapon of deadly effectiveness: the serpent of fire, that is, a lightning flash with which he cut off his sister's head

Fig. 16 Huitzilopochtli carries in his hand the famous serpent of fire. Borbónico codex. Drawing by A. Villagra.

and killed his innumerable brothers. This prodigious warrior was no less than the god Huitzilopochtli.

It is curious to observe how this story of the birth and of the infinite power of the serpent of fire was kept alive and profoundly believed. In 1521, during the final days of the defense of the Mexica capital against Cortez, Cuauhtemoc decided that the moment had arrived to resort to his supreme weapon. He implored the god Huitzilopochtli and dressed a young brave warrior in the clothes of an ancient emperor known as a mighty, victorious general. And above all he put in his hand the weapon of the god, with which he would be able to vanquish the Spaniards. He went into the battle, but after a slight skirmish in which he only succeeded in taking prisoners, he had to retreat. The divine weapon had failed. The conquest was then inevitable.

But, returning to the myth of the birth of Huitzilopochtli, the widow signifies the earth from which all things are born; the daughter is the moon and the "four hundred" sons are the stars which pale and disappear completely with the rising Sun, represented by the god Huitzilopochtli. Since he was the god of the Mexica, his identification with the Sun is of prime importance, for he converted them into the "People of the Sun," as Alfonso Caso has brilliantly stated.

They were therefore the representatives of the Sun on the Earth and responsible for keeping it alive. This high office and obligation was a decisive factor in their history and clarifies many episodes.

* * * *

The end of the twelfth century and the first years of the thirteenth witnessed an interminable series of small Chichimec invasions which were only the prelude to the great invasion of 1224 by the Chichimecs who were called "those of Xolotl." The latter seem to have come from a region neighboring on the Valley of the Mezquital. Their chief, Xolotl, launched them along a course of conquests which was, as in all similar cases, to lead to the formation of a new dynasty and a new empire upon the ruins of past ones. In the pictorial manuscripts, Xolotl's group appears as hunters dressed in deer hides and living in caves.

"When our ancestors settled here, the first ones, who came to rule the uncultivated land of weeds and trees—the *páramo* (high wasteland)—the goods they brought with them were quails, snakes, rabbits, and deer, and they ate them during their years and days of wanderings. They were a good example to the others for they raised and preserved their peoples and their dominion with the sole help of Ipalnemoani, because the Lord of the World lives in all things." In a few years they seem to have taken possession of a great part of the Valley of Mexico, and after another effort established their capital in a new site called Tenayuca. In this place they erected a pyramid that would be continually enlarged by their successors. It is very important today, because it is the only Chichimec monument in the Valley of Mexico that we know thoroughly. It takes many of its architectural elements from older temples, but it does introduce at least one very economical idea: the placing of two separate temples on a single base. In the first periods, an enormous flight of steps led up to the two sanctuaries. Later it was separated in two equal sections by a broad balustrade. In this form each of the temples preserved its independence and had the same importance. One of them was dedicated to the principal representative of the ancient civilizations, Tlaloc, god of the rain; the other to the great Toltec-Chichimec god, Tezcatlipoca.

The temple of Tenayuca, skillfully explored and in part reconstructed a few years ago, is an interesting place to visit in the outskirts of Mexico City (Plate 15). Its numerous superstructures are each built in the same way: a stone and earth nucleus with smaller stones as veneer, covered in turn by a thick coating of stucco. Apart from the magnitude of the building itself, one admires the splendid serpents and heads that encircle it, and which, following in part the tradition begun in Tula, form the "wall of serpents." About eight hundred snakes of different forms and sizes have been found in Tenayuca.

Fig. 17 Mexica sculpture depicting Tlaloc. Drawing by A. Mendoza.

Undoubtedly, the building was devoted to solar worship, especially to the setting sun: the dying sun which so obsessed the Indian soul. This aspect of solar worship, as well as the wall of serpents or the two temples placed on a single base, were imitated centuries later in Tenochtitlán, although there the proportions were much more generous. Tlaloc continued reigning in one of the temples, but in the other we find Huitzilopochtli instead of Tezcatlipoca, for in the great Mexica temple their own god naturally must have the principal position. This change is, in reality, less than one might imagine on first glance since Huitzilopochtli is no other than a Tezcatlipoca of a more recent vintage.

Despite all the construction that began with this sanctuary at Tenayuca, Xolotl was still fundamentally a nomad and therefore constantly changed his residence. The chronicles tell us that his people did not sow, which is not at all certain. They did not plant corn but did grow some other grains. Although basically hunters, they supplemented the hunt, at that time very scarce in the Valley of Mexico, with temporary crops, which did not necessarily demand fixed quarters in a determined place.

Xolotl was a new Mixcoatl. The usual sources depict him as another ever-victorious conqueror and the terror of the peoples surrounding him. The two might easily be compared to Genghis Khan; they are an avalanche thundering down from the steppes, an Attila on foot, crushing everything before them. In addition, Xolotl as well as Mix-

Fig. 18 Xolotl according to the Xolotl codex. Drawing by A. Villagra.

coatl were the first to use the bow and arrow in Middle
America, a much more efficient weapon than the *atlatl* of
the old sedentary peoples.

If Xolotl did not have the luck to procreate a son as
illustrious as Quetzalcoatl, his son did initiate a line which
reigned almost uninterruptedly until the Spanish conquest.
In addition to retaining the Chichimec throne, his descendants were intermingled with all the reigning families.
Among his offspring was another of the most extraordinary
figures of ancient Mexico, Netzahualcoyotl, the poet-king
of Texcoco.

The remnants of the Toltecs were suffering countless
persecutions at the hands of the new dominating people.
In a very picturesque form the Chichimec-Toltec history
recounts the way in which by civilizing the Chichimecs
they came upon an easy life:

"In one year the settlers caused great suffering among
the Toltecs, because they wished to destroy them. So the
Toltecs implored their god and master, weeping with sad-
ness and tribulation and said to him: 'Our Lord Master
of the World, through whom everything lives, our Creator
and Maker, will you no longer afford us your protection
here? The Xochimilcas and the Ayapancas are troubling
us sorely because they wish to destroy our people. You
know very well that we are not many. Let us not perish
at the hands of our enemies. Have mercy on us, your vassals, and keep war away. Staunch god, hear our lament.
Let us not be destroyed. Rather, let the power of our enemies be crushed and their people and their domain, their
nobility and their subjects perish.' And then he answered
and they listened to a voice which said to them: 'Do not
be sad and do not cry. I already know all. Now I tell you,
Icxicouatl and Quetzalteueyac, go to the hills of Colhuaca;
there are the Chichimecs, the great heroes and conquerors.
They will destroy your enemies the Xochimilcas and the
Ayapancas. Do not cry. Go before the Chichimecs and implore them insistently. Do exactly as I say. All this I command you to do.'"

After six days of marching they reached the hill of

Culhuacán and found the Chichimecs inside the cave. After a series of magic rites the Toltec ambassador got the Chichimecs to come out with their interpreter, who was needed since they spoke a different language. The ambassador immediately said: "Listen, Couatzin [the inter-

Fig. 19 Scenes from Chichimec life: deer hunting, a cave. Quinatzin codex. Drawings by A. Villagra.

preter], we come to lead you away from your cave and mountain life." After the conversation was over, both parties raised a chant almost unintelligible to us, and the Chichimecs at last understood the heart of the message. It consisted of proposing an agreement with them whereby the Toltecs would civilize the Chichimecs and the latter would aid in the war against the oppressors. "They seek us out," they said, "because of their war, and the hardened shaft and the shield are our fate and our destiny." When the conference was over, the Toltec ambassadors consecrated the Chichimec chieftains by perforating the septum of their noses in the traditional manner with a bone of an eagle and of a jaguar. And the chronicle says, "Here end the roads and the days."

This extraordinary transaction, in which each part exchanged the products it possessed—the Toltecs, civilization; and the Chichimecs, armed force—led in time to magnificent results. We observe the fusion of two forces, tradition and newness, to produce the Mexica empire.

Indeed, this process which the Indian chronicle tells us in magical and simplified form unfolded during the thirteenth and fourteenth centuries. And it reminds us of what had happened to the Nonoalcas in Tula. Surrounded by the older sedentary peoples whom they had conquered without causing them to disappear, the Chichimecs gradually absorbed the old Toltec culture. It is the typical example of Greece and Rome.

This fusion was accelerated by the arrival, under the reign of Tlotzin, Xolotl's nephew, of a series of more cultured immigrants who brought with them ancient knowledge. The most interesting are those whom the chronicles name "Those Who Returned." They were probably a people who had lived in the valley, immigrated to Mixtec lands where they acquired the very refined culture of that people, and then returned to the Valley of Mexico; and so the name by which we know them. Possibly these "Returners" are responsible for the fine Mexica gold and silverwork, a direct descendant of Mixtec style, as well as the art of painting hieroglyphics and historical books,

Fig. 20 Cultivated plants. Tlotzin codex. Drawings by A. Villagra.

which was so developed in this Oaxacan region. It is said that these immigrants, together with others who arrived in this period, erected the first houses of Texcoco around 1327 and introduced agriculture, pottery, and many other improvements to a Chichimec group. Because of the rise at this time in the level of the lakes, the *chinampas* (garden patches amid lakes) became again an important source of agricultural products.

The changes caused a schism, for one faction of the Chichimecs who were more reactionary than the others refused to accept these new developments and tried to take over; but they were defeated and from then on the more advanced group predominated. A century later, under the distinguished reign of Netzahualcoyotl, they made the Chichimec monarchy the very center of Indian culture, which in time earned Texcoco the name of the "American Athens."

To reach this glorious moment the Chichimec monarchy was—like Spain of the Catholic kings—a monarchy without a fixed capital. Only toward the middle of the fourteenth century did they settle definitively in Texcoco, becoming again sedentary. But before continuing with the history of these Chichimecs, we must study at least in a cursory manner some of the main groups which had settled at different dates in the Valley of Mexico. Without doing this, we should find the events from the thirteenth to the sixteenth centuries to be unintelligible.

During the time of the Chichimec supremacy, one last stronghold remained in the Valley of Mexico—Culhuacán, where the vanquished Toltecs had come to find refuge. There, during the thirteenth century and part of the fourteenth, a dynasty reigned which, legitimately or not, claimed direct descent from the Tula kings and therefore from Quetzalcoatl. They owed their prestige to this. Besides, they cleverly took full advantage of a situation which made it an imperative for other rulers to have Toltec blood. We shall see that the leaders of each new group entering the valley desired a chieftain or a wife from the house of Culhuacán. For the lords of Culhuacán, these dynastic alliances allowed at least a shadow of independence.

* * * *

We left the Mexicans in Tula, transforming their god into the sun. Yet not even this divine metamorphosis improved their situation very quickly. So we see them going from place to place until after 1215 they arrived in the Valley of Mexico, where they continued changing their domicile. In general, they were badly received everywhere, and after settling for a short while were thrown out because their behavior was insufferable to their neighbors. Rapidly, they acquired a well-deserved reputation of being quarrelsome, cruel, unfaithful to their word, and women-stealers. On the other hand, they were known as extremely brave. "The Mexicans supported themselves solely by means of war and they disdained death," as the Annals of Tlaltelolco say.

The *History of Tlaltelolco from the Most Remote Times* mentions their poverty and primitive simplicity:

"Their garments and loincloths were of palm fiber, their sandals of woven straw as were their bows, their sacks." The description of the Mexicans on this cultural level reminds us of the nomads in the north of Mesoamerica where until the sixteenth century the way of life scarcely changed, for they did not participate in the civilization which reached to their southern border. The discovery of the Cave of the Candelaria, near Torreón, has revealed a few objects probably similar to those used by the Mexica during the period of their peregrinations. Indeed, things of wood or cloth were preserved in the Candelaria which dampness destroyed in other places: fiber sandals; bows or dart-shooters; stone knives with painted wood handles; nets used as sacks; thick, colored blankets in which they wrapped the dead.

We do not know quite how, but at last they managed to settle at Chapultepec, where thanks to the strategic value of the site they remained a good many years, possibly until a date which varies between 1299 and 1323. This famous, strategic hill, where years later the Mexican emperors had their portraits engraved on the bare rock, where the Spanish viceroys built a mansion, where the heroic defense of the Niños Heroes took place, where Maximilian left a splendid palace, is today the Museum of Mexican History, and very justly so. Here the Mexicans knew the first years of relative tranquillity.

After this move, their culture was more advanced and complete. They had learned something of farming techniques, even some of the most advanced methods such as those of the *chinampas*. At moments of crisis they returned to their original poverty, but they were acquainted with the civilization of their neighbors, even though they did not adopt it. So we know that they already had painted books, a calendar, cyclical fiestas, and even stone constructions, however elementary they may have been. But Huitzilopochtli kept vigil, and succeeded in making them increasingly odious to their neighbors until a coalition was formed against them led by the Tepanecs and the people of Culhuacán. By means of treachery, the allies got the men to come out of their fortification and at this moment fell upon the women and children. The Mexicans, demoralized, were conquered and carried off as prisoners. Their chief, Huitzilihuitl the Elder, was sacrificed in Culhuacán and the others became captives of the Culhuas.

An ancient poem narrates this episode:

> The margin of the earth was shattered
> sorrowful omens hovered above us
> the sky split open above us
> and upon us in Chapultepec
> he came down for whom All lives.
>
> . . . . . .
>
> They are right to say
> that Mexicans no longer exist
> that no place left has the root of the sky
> and he for Whom all lives says:
> "although you are no longer great, do not cry"
> He will not be parted from his creatures.
>
> Then why does he remain remote?
> His heart cries, for his subjects will perish
> With our shield twisted to every side
> we perished in Chapultepec
> I the Mexican.
> The Culhua was bathed in glory, the Tepaneca
>   was bathed in glory.
> The Mexicans were carried off as slaves
> in four directions.
> The chief Huitzilihuitl was appalled
> when they placed the sacrificial flag in his
>   hand at Culhuacán
> But the Mexicans who escaped from enemy hands
> the old ones waded to the center of the water
> where the bulrush and reeds were whispering.
>
> . . . . . .

Later Ocelopan the Mexican says:

> How happy are the noble lords Acolnauacatl
>   and Tezozomoctli,

who won this land with penitent armies
perhaps the word of the princes of Azcapotzalco
may not be favorable
O I hope that Tepanecatl will not carry off
    your sons
to the land of the dead
and that hostility and blood will not come upon us.

Shortly after the terrible defeat at Chapultepec, King Achitometl of Culhuacán gave them lands in Tizapán with the secret hope that the countless snakes in this place would destroy the Mexicans. But, ironically, the chronicle tells us that "the Mexicans rejoiced greatly as soon as they saw the snakes and they roasted and cooked them all and ate them all up." When the emissaries of the king of Culhuacán told him this, he replied disconsolately: "You see what rascals they are; do not bother with them or even talk to them."

Despite the attraction of such a delicious feast, the Mexicans did not remain long in Tizapán. Their god kept vigil and would not permit them to settle amid the relative luxury of the banquet of snakes.

According to the *Mexicayotl Chronicle*, Huitzilopochtli told them: "Hear me, we will not remain here but go where we shall find those whom we shall capture and dominate. But we will not make the mistake of being nice to the Culhuacáns. We will begin a war. I order this. Go and ask Achitometl for his offspring, his virgin daughter, his own dearly-loved child; I know and I shall give her to you." Instantly, the Mexicans went to ask Achitometl for his virgin daughter. They begged him for her saying, "We all supplicate you to concede us your necklace, your Quetzal plumes, your young virgin daughter—your noble princess whom we shall keep in Tizapán." And Achitometl at once replied: "Very well, O Mexicans, take her away." As soon as they arrived in Tizapán Huitzilopochtli said: "Kill and skin the daughter of Achitometl, I order you, and when you have skinned her dress some priest in her flesh. Then go call on Achitometl." The Mexicans did as ordered, and having accepted the invitation, Achitometl came with rubber, incense, paper, tobacco, and foods to offer to the god. He placed his gift at the feet of the supposed god who was in a dark room. But on lighting the fire to burn the incense, he realized that the god was no other than a priest dressed in the skin of his daughter. Immediately he cried out to his co-princes and his subjects saying: "What is the matter with you, O Culhuacáns! Do you not see that they have skinned my daughter! Let those scoundrels be gone! Let us kill and destroy those who have come here!"

The consequence of this horrible story is naturally another war in which the Mexicans were expelled from Tizapán. Since no one wished to accept them, they found it necessary to take refuge on the water, in the marshes, to hide among the reeds. Terrible and immutable Huitzilopochtli continued ordering all that they were to do. The almost aquatic life of this people at this time permitted the priests of the god to give their supreme order, the most adroit of all they had pronounced: the foundation of Tenochtitlán upon an island. Insignificant at the beginning, this event was to have the greatest repercussions upon the future of Mexico.

The *Mexicayotl Chronicle* narrates this episode in poetic form. It tells us that while they were exiled, with no place to set up the temple of their god, Huitzilopochtli came to them again and ordered them to continue their search until they found the exact place which from the beginning of time he had marked for the foundation of the Mexican capital. "Within the reed fields he would stand tall and watch over them, and so he ordered the Mexicans. At once they saw the *ahuehuete*, the white willow tree that grows there and the reed and the white rush and the frog and the white fish and the white water snake, and then they saw that there was a cave. Upon seeing this the old men wept and said: 'Here is where the place must be, for we have seen what our priest Huitzilopochtli told us and ordered.' Then Huitzilopochtli spoke again: 'Hear me, for there is something else that you have not yet seen. Go at once to see the Tenoch, on which you will see an eagle happily resting, sunning himself there, and you should be pleased, for this is where the heart of Copil was born. We shall find ourselves equipped with arrow and shield, and conquer and seize all those who surround us, for here will be our Mexican homeland, the place where the eagle screams and spreads his wings and eats, the place where the fish swims, the place where the serpent is torn apart and many things will happen.' And when they arrived at the place, they saw the eagle perched upon the nopal happily eating and tearing apart his food, and as soon as the eagle saw them he lowered his head. Although they saw him from very far, they saw that his nest was made of various precious feathers, and saw the heads of all kinds of birds scattered about. And at once the inhabitants wept because of this, and said: 'We are rewarded, we have attained our desire since we have seen and marveled at the place where our new settlement will be. Let us go there and rest.' Then Tlachiuhtetelli and his Tlalmomoztli settled there. And so, abjectly poor and miserable, they made the house of Huitzilopochtli. When they built the said oratory, it was still small, because they were still on outlying land when they came to settle among the rushes and the reeds from which they had to take stone and wood. And since these were lands of the Tepanecs as well as the Texcocans who lived at the Culhuacán border, they suffered greatly from all that. All this occurred in the year 'two-house' (1325) after the birth of our Savior Jesus Christ, and it was then that the ancient Mexica entered, arrived and settled in the reed fields and the rushes, in the water of Tenochtitlán."

The settling of Tenochtitlán is not only the most characteristic episode in all Mexica history but the one which best reveals their way of being, that combination of practical intelligence and political acumen mixed with fanaticism and disdain for suffering.

Here it is interesting to note, in the first place, the apparently absurd but actually extraordinary selection which the priests had made for the site in which they would found their city. A small islet, almost a marshland from which a few rocks jutted, surrounded by reed fields on the lake of Texcoco. It was a very unattractive site which no one of the innumerable former inhabitants of the valley had occupied. The brilliant Mexica leaders must have understood the strategic and political value of the site. As an island, its defense was very easy since one could only attack it by water. Moreover, it was situated on the borders of three kingdoms and, actually because of being next to all three, it was subject to no one of them. This gave the new settlers a position of relative independence and permitted them to side with any one of their neighbors against the others.

In the course of the following century they were to take full advantage of this flexible position and we shall see them as mercenaries of Azcapotzalco attacking the others, then allying themselves with Texcoco to defeat the Tepanecs; and so they continued until they rose above the others, always preserving their city free from enemy attacks. Unfortunately, it is not possible for us to know to what extent the priest-chieftains, who spoke through the mouth of their god, were aware of all these advantages. But it is evident that through all their history of wandering, although perhaps confusedly, they sought a similar site, a "promised land," and that they were determined, by whatever means, to bring their people into hegemony over the valleys.

With time the island was to offer another great advantage; this was commercial in nature. The transportation system which prevailed in ancient Mexico was so primitive that it could only make use of *man* as a beast of burden. Since the wheel never was more than a toy, there was never any kind of drawn vehicle. Under these conditions the transport of merchandise, especially when a matter of feeding a great city, became practically an insoluble problem. A single canoe, however, with little power, could do the work of many men for several days. This factor surely is one of the causes of the extraordinary development which

soon took place in Tenochtitlán. Again, the lake seemed
to dictate the Mexican destiny.

Their other weapon was austerity and fanaticism. For
centuries the people were never allowed to remain permanently in one place, were obliged to move constantly,
and this prevented an accumulation of wealth, the benefit
of cultivated lands, or the adoption of lazy and luxurious
habits. The Mexica men were internally prepared for war
or for sacrifice, precisely because they had so little to lose,
because their life was far from being comfortable. The very
poverty of their chosen sites forced them to try continually
to get from their richer neighbors all those things which
they did not have, and, if they could not do this by force,
then to work unceasingly to obtain those things through
trade. So we see, for example, that shortly after the city
was founded they directed their efforts to gathering a great
quantity of fish, shrimp, amphibians, and other lake products to barter for wood or stone in order to build the temple of their god, even before their own houses. Work,
austerity, fanaticism.

Now it is time to ask ourselves who is that Huitzilopochtli who for centuries led his people, turning them into
a "chosen people." In the chronicles he always appears as
the supreme god whose voice the priests listened to with
trembling and reverence. We are evidently dealing with
a very small group—no more than four persons—of ruling
priests who used the artifice of the divine voice to guide
their people and shape the destiny of the Mexicans. The
interesting aspect of this situation is that from the beginning of their history one has the impression of a clear and
truly established program, a program which developed
across the centuries; a brutal but ingenious conception of
government which, followed relentlessly by the small in-
domitable elite, carried their people through thousands of
dangers, privations, and sacrifices until they obtained the
ultimate triumph, the empire. The people were driven
without thought of hunger or fatigue; and with women
and children dying they pitted all their strength against
any resistance, toward the goal which this elite had prom-

ised them. Of course, it is impossible to think that the same leaders could have molded and followed this almost diabolical plan through such a long span of time. But the first ones set the pattern which was followed by their descendants until the end. Huitzilopochtli spoke indefatigably on all important occasions as the cruelest yet most agile politician. He never wearied, never halted; nothing satisfied him. For fifteen generations, his dreadful voice bore down on the people with tragic advice for violent action, without a minute of respite.

The triumph, very much later, was to signify for Huitzilopochtli, as for all peoples who triumph brutally, the beginning of the end. At the high point of Mexican power, we no longer hear his forceful voice thundering through the chronicles. The small group of priests had already become an extensive aristocracy which could not have the original force nor cohesiveness. The empire and the wealth must have corroded the unbreakable will of those first times.

The culminating moment in the history of those ingenious, terrible priests, the moment we best see them use their brilliant intelligence, is precisely at the founding of the city.

They knew that for a people like theirs, this site of Tenochtitlán alone, despised by all the rest, provided them with the possibility of attaining their ambitions—to become a great power. They began by understanding that only if forced to, would the Mexicans live on that small, marshy island. Perhaps for this reason they forced the performance of that drama which was to cost the life of the daughter of Achitometl of Culhuacán. After this, there was no question of choosing, there remained only the lake, the eternal center of the fate of ancient Mexico. But the physical compulsion was not enough; a moral compulsion was needed. So it happened that upon settling on the lake the prophecies were fulfilled, for they discovered on the lake, quite according to plan, the famous eagle on the *tuna*, above a rock, eating the serpent in the same place where the heart of Copil had been cast.

Once having settled on the island and built the first temple to their god, which was only a shabby structure that would disappear in the radiant future, the Mexicans understood that it was not possible to move too quickly. They were not even masters of the small island in which they had taken refuge. Taking advantage of their foremost virtues, bravery and military prowess, they became mercenaries of the nearest power to them, which at this time was the Tepanecs who ruled over Azcapotzalco. The latter imposed upon them the obligation to help in time of war and also exacted a number of tributes, at times excessive, in exchange for their protection. They were therefore part mercenaries and part tributaries of the Tepanecs. The Tepanecs often asked impossible tributes in order to offend them. For example, they had to bring the Tepanecs ducks from the lagoon who would lay their eggs at the moment of being delivered.

In 1367, still in league with Azcapotzalco, they destroyed Culhuacán, the last center of some importance, where, as a true historical survival, men ruled who considered themselves Toltecs. This event had future importance, for it left open "the Toltec succession" which the Mexicans were later to claim for themselves. In 1371 the other Mexican faction, the Tlatelolcas, took Tenayuca while also in the service of Azcapotzalco. The victory was at the expense of the Chichimec lords of Texcoco.

Five years later, they thought themselves important enough to have a king, as their cohorts in Tlatelolco already had. Then with shrewd political instinct they did not ask for an heir from the reigning house of Azcapotzalco, obviously the stronger power. They elected a descendant from the deposed king of Culhuacán. This first lord of the Mexicans was called Acamapichtli. This selection, at first glance insignificant, was to give them a certain right to claim the Toltec succession as their own, since the Culhuacáns were considered the legitimate heirs of the old kings. They were to cultivate this idea and this vague right in such a fruitful way that one hundred years later the Mexicans became masters not only of almost all the

Toltec empire but of an even more extensive territory. All the while they laid claim to an ancestral heritage.

But this glorious future was still in the mind of the gods. For the moment Acamapichtli, dominated by Azcapotzalco, plunged into a very long war against the people of the Morelos valley, a war which ended only many years after his death and whose episodes we shall relate presently.

* * * *

We have referred often to the Tepanecs of Azcapotzalco. Now we must go back in time to study this group which was to be so prominent on the political scene until the second decade of the fifteenth century. Coming originally from the Valley of Toluca, this people had preserved to a high degree the Toltec civilization, for the region appears not to have been invaded during the chaotic century that followed the fall of Tula. Once in the valley, they established their capital on a site that had become an epilogue of Teotihuacán civilization: Azcapotzalco, today a section in northeast Mexico City. This event happened about 1230. For a little more than a century Azcapotzalco progressed slowly under a series of obscure kings. But around 1363 an extraordinary man occupied the throne, Tezozomoc, under whose rule, which lasted until 1426, Azcapotzalco became the most important city of the valley.

Tezozomoc's long reign was marked by an interminable series of wars. We have already noted that by using the Mexicans as mercenaries he conquered Culhuacán. This victory whet the Tepanec ambition for the whole south of the valley and the future possibilities of crossing into the plains of Morelos. We also have seen how they conquered Tenayuca, until a short time before the capital of the Chichimec lords until that time. This new conquest awakened their appetite to the possibility of finally swallowing up the entire ancient Xolotl empire. Indeed, with one moment of truce and another of war, Tezozomoc never wavered an instant from his course until, long afterwards, he achieved a total triumph.

But in order to obtain these ends, he had to consolidate his position in the southern region of the Valley of Mexico and absorb a sizable group of independent domains. These we have not noted here so as not to make this history even more confused; yet these smaller political areas gave the Central Valleys in the thirteenth and the greater part of the fourteenth centuries a feudal character based on a network of small principalities in continual struggle with each other, in alliances and new struggles. This situation recalls Italy at a similar period where we see the same internal, vain game of alliances, changeable as sand, of sterile battles and ephemeral victories.

Having seized control of the entire central part of the valley between Culhuacán and Tenayuca, Tezozomoc could pursue his course to the north or to the south. In the latter direction we have noted that he launched his mercenaries like an arrowhead into the Morelos region. In the north the Xaltocan power on the one side and the Chichimec on the other were isolated and ready to be conquered. Xaltocan fell around 1400. Then the only remaining task was to complete the conquest of Texcoco and its empire.

This empire had been divided into dominions, which made the task easier. Thus, we see them fall one by one. When Ixtlilxochitl ascended to the throne of Texcoco, probably in 1409, the situation was already desperate and his nine years of rule passed amid continual crises and false promises of peace on the part of Tezozomoc.

The problem was present from the first days of his reign. In 1410 Ixtlilxochitl convoked the ceremony for taking the oath of office as the Chichimec sovereign. Only two lords attended the ceremony, according to his historian and descendant of the same name. The others excused themselves on the pretext of guarding the frontiers. But the most ominous absence at this ceremony was that of the old tyrant Tezozomoc, who not only refused to attend but laid claim to the right of succession since both kings were descendants of Xolotl. He sent a messenger to Ixtlilxochitl carrying the supreme insult: a load of raw cotton that was to be returned to him as woven blankets. According to Indian custom, this meant that he considered Ixtlilxochitl a weak woman who was capable only of weaving cotton. The problem was crucial for Ixtlilxochitl: if he returned the cotton with insulting words, thus maintaining his dignity, it meant immediate war with Tezozomoc. Ixtlilxochitl had neither armies nor a supply of weapons. So he submitted to gain time. He ordered soldiers recruited, arms made, and he concentrated in the center of his country all his forces, which until that time were scattered across his distant possessions.

So at the beginning, the claims of the Tepanec king did not seem to be successful, and Ixtlilxochitl took power despite his rival. He married a sister of Chimalpopoca of Mexico, a granddaughter indeed of Tezozomoc, and began to rule.

In 1414 Ixtlilxochitl saw clearly that the situation was becoming increasingly desperate. He decided in that year to have his son Netzahualcoyotl take the oath as heir to the throne. With this he hoped to obtain two advantages: to save, if not his own reign, at least the future rights of his dynasty, and to know which lords were still loyal to him. It was difficult to determine this without a ceremony that would clearly distinguish each one's allegiance, for now Tezozomoc was using not only war but cunning, treason, alliances, and even corruption to acquire friendships in the rival camp.

Ixtlilxochitl proclaimed a day of assembly for all the chiefs near Huexotla. They would meet in a great plain where he had built a throne. When the day arrived, the pompous ceremony unfolded according to the old Toltec rites; but very few important personages were present, since the majority preferred not to attend out of fear of Tezozomoc.

With the lamentable result of this meeting began the final agony of Ixtlilxochitl's reign. The king managed to begin another campaign with his new army. Victorious at the beginning, for he was invading Azcapotzalco's lands, he even defeated Tezozomoc, who sued for peace, according to the chronicler (who was very partial to Ixtlilxochitl and therefore difficult to accept entirely). The king accepted, considered the war over, and ordered his army dissolved. But the fact is that in 1418 Tezozomoc's troops were at the gates of Texcoco: many of his former enemies had come over to his side and Ixtlilxochitl found himself almost alone.

Accompanied by his son Netzahualcoyotl and surrounded by the last of the faithful, he made a stronghold in the forest where upon seeing himself lost he withdrew to a deep ravine. Below a great fallen tree he spent the night in the company of his son and two captains. At sunrise the next day, a soldier came to tell him that the enemy knew where he was and that armed men were coming with great speed in order to kill him. Then he asked the soldiers to leave him alone, called his son and said to him: "My dearly loved son, lion's arm, Netzahualcoyotl, where can I take you to find some debtor or relative to take you in? Here will be the last day of my misfortunes. I am forced to depart from this life. I beg and entrust you not to forsake your subjects and vassals, not to forget that you are a Chichimec, to recover your empire which Tezozomoc has so unjustly stolen, and to avenge the death of your afflicted father. You will make use of bow and arrow. Now you must simply hide in this grove, because your innocent death would bring to an end the very ancient empire of your ancestors." After this touching scene the small prince hid among the branches and saw how the enemy slaughtered his father. Once they were gone, he recovered the body and aided by some friends prepared the corpse and burnt it. Ixtlilxochitl was the first Chichimec emperor cremated according to the Toltec rites and ceremonies, instead of being buried in a cave as were his ancestors.

With the death of Ixtlilxochitl began the "government in exile" of the Chichimec dynasty in the person of the young Netzahualcoyotl, the Fasting Coyote, the legitimate heir of the empire. This boy, whose youth was so unfortunate, was to become the most illustrious figure of his century. For the moment he had to take refuge in one place or another, followed implacably by the hatred of Tezozomoc who wished to see him disappear, for he was the only legitimate rival that remained. A while later he settled in Tlaxcala and at times at the court of his uncle Chimalpopoca of Mexico.

The chronicles tell us of innumerable episodes in the adventures of Netzahualcoyotl during his exile. They were more or less true. Dangers did not stop him, as his descendant said, from going "to all parts of the land without omitting a single domain, city, province, and town in order to know the intentions and will of the lords of these places. In some they received him with great joy; in others very secretly, warning him to be on guard against his enemies. At times he went disguised and heard what they said about him, thus ascertaining the opinion of the local masters and the orders of Tezozomoc." His presence so obsessed the tyrant that it is even said that he dreamed of him three times. "The first time he dreamed of him as a royal eagle that clawed his head and seemed to rip out his entrails and heart and tore off his legs." In the midst of countless adventures, always eluding the wrath of Tezozomoc, protected at times by his wits and at others by important relatives, the young Netzahualcoyotl waited with bitterness as the years of exile passed by. But while he had youth which allowed him to hope, his rival, Tezozomoc, was increasingly sick, not from disease but from old age: "And as he appears in the stories and as the leading old men declared to me, he was so old that they carried him like a baby among feathers and loving furs and always took him out in the sun to warm him up, and at night he slept between two braziers of strong fire and that he was never removed from the heat because he lacked natural warmth." As one might expect in these circumstances, the tyrant died at last in 1426 and a wind of independence swept through the valley.

The long reign of Tezozomoc, sixty-three years, had an importance much greater than the simple consolidation of Tepanec supremacy. Since the now remote days of the fall of Tula, Tezozomoc was the first one who succeeded in uniting under his direct or indirect rule, by means of his fivefold alliance, the whole Valley of Mexico, a great part of the surrounding valleys, and even more distant lands. His troops had reached the region of Taxco. This marked the end of the innumerable small dominions into which the lands had been divided as a consequence of the Toltec dispersion. The Tepanecs in a certain sense had the honor of putting an end to this situation. On uniting these semi-independent fiefs, they prepared the way for the larger unification which the Mexica would accomplish. But Tezozomoc governed a group that was not really local, for they spoke Matlatzinca instead of Nahuatl and their roots were not deep. This was the profound weakness of his empire, and though hidden during his brilliant reign, it became abundantly clear after his death. Tezozomoc's extraordinary intelligence, aided by his perfidy and total lack of scruples, was complemented with the good fortune of a very long life. All this allowed him to carry his work to its intended end. In this way he achieved an incomparable prestige, but his work, like all works of violence, could not endure.

He not only used war as an instrument of expansion but resorted to a tortuous strategy of alliances and betrayals which helped him seize numerous places that he could not have conquered with military power alone or whose conquest might have forced him into long-drawn-out campaigns. He reinforced his action by entering systematically into dynastic alliances. In time he married off many of his children and grandchildren to the heirs of almost all the domains in the Valley of Mexico. Through his widely dispersed family he intervened in the affairs of all the cities and became the indisputable lord of the region.

Unfortunately, we have very few data on this figure, whom it would be very interesting to know more thoroughly. He appears and disappears fleetingly in the chronicles. But the little we do know of his personality makes us think that, much better than Caesar Borgia, he might have served as a model for Machiavelli's *The Prince*.

He left in the minds of his political successors a new formula in the art of governing, a formula admirably adapted to the character of the Mexicans who, as Jiménez

Moreno says, "learned their lessons in the school of Tezozomoc of Azcapotzalco." We shall soon see them brilliantly applying those principles of brutal realism. But before this, we must go back to examine what had happened in Tenochtitlán during the years of Tepanec splendor.

At the death of the leader Acamapichtli, his son Huitzilihuitl ascended to the throne. Because of the continued ties with Tezozomoc, he fought victoriously against several peoples in the valley, and above all continued the struggle against the people of the Morelos Valley, who were captained by the lord of Cuernavaca. During a lull between battles, the *Mexicayotl Chronicle* tells us how Huitzilihuitl fell in love with the daughter of the lord of Cuernavaca. "His heart was in Cuernavaca, there alone, and he immediately sent word to her parents asking for her hand."

But the young girl's father was a witch doctor: "He called on all the spiders as well as the centipede, the serpent, the bat and the scorpion, ordering all of them to guard his very famous virgin daughter so that no one might enter there and no villain dishonor her. She was locked in and well guarded, with every species of wild beast at all the palace doors. Because of this there was great fear and no one approached the palace. The kings of all the towns solicited this princess, because they wished to marry her with their sons. But the father accepted none of the proposals." As soon as the lord of Cuernavaca heard that the lord of Mexico was seeking his daughter he said to his envoys, "What does he say? What can he give her?—that which the water yields, that is, will he dress her as he is attired in clothing made from linen of the waters? And what foods will he give her? Or is his home possibly like this where there is everything, meats and delicious fruits, the indispensable cotton and elegant garments? Go tell all this to your king before you return here." Huitzilihuitl was downcast upon learning that his proposal had been rejected, and then in dreams the god Tezcatlipoca appeared to him, saying, "Do not grieve, for I have come to tell you what you must do in order to win the virgin.

Make a spear and a small net and with them you will go to the house of the lord of Cuernavaca where his daughter is kept under guard. Make also a beautiful staff. Decorate it carefully, paint it well, inserting in the center a precious stone, shining handsomely. You must go there along the borders where you will cast the cane in the center of which is the precious stone, and it will fall to earth where the daughter of the king of Cuernavaca is being protected and then we shall have her." The lover did exactly what the god had proposed, and when the staff fell the virgin saw it descending through the sky, and she took it and broke it in the center and saw inside the precious stone. Very femininely she wished to be certain that the stone was good and she bit it. But she swallowed it and then could not get it out, so that she found herself pregnant. Since the lord of Mexico was the cause of her pregnancy, her father offered her to him as his wife.

In reading the chronicle carefully, we realize that this page of love is considerably less romantic than it seems to be at first glance. Actually, just as the young girl revealed her monetary interest by biting the stone to see if it was genuine, the true motive of the lord of Mexico was not so much passion as the desire to obtain the rich cotton production of the Morelos region and to retaliate on just that score for which his future father-in-law reproached him—of being dressed in clothing woven from water plants. From that time onward cotton clothing could be obtained in the Tlatelolco market.

At Huitzilihuitl's death in 1417 he was followed by Chimalpopoca, a grandson by his mother of Tezozomoc of Azcapotzalco.

This tie was very advantageous to the Mexicans, for the new king's grandfather reduced the tributes from them. It was probably Chimalpopoca's kinship with Tezozomoc that raised him to the supreme rank, for he was scarcely twelve years old when he became king. The ten years of his reign were quite unimportant in Mexican annals. In 1426 old Tezozomoc died weighed down with years and glory, and a war broke out between his two sons, for both claimed to be his heir apparent.

Chimalpopoca committed the worst error that a governor could make: He aided the brother who was losing the battle. The victor, Maxtla, ordered the death of most of his brother's partisans who had conspired against him. Chimalpopoca was imprisoned and it appears that he was hanged at the age of twenty-two. With the death of Tezozomoc and the inglorious end of his grandchild Chimalpopoca, we reach the most important moment in Mexican history, when a new period began which would bring Tenochtitlán into hegemony over the Central Valleys.

IX. THE MEXICA

In 1427 the Mexica elected a new king, Itzcoatl, who was the son of Acamapichtli, the first Mexican king, and of a slavewoman. This was the only case in which a man ascended to the throne whose mother was not of Toltec blood. The election was due, surely, to the exceptional qualities of the candidate, whose military genius and political skill were to transform the fate of his people during the thirteen years of his reign.

By reason of the quarrel between the sons of Tezozomoc, the various "governments in exile," brought about by Tezozomoc's conquests, understood that this was the moment to return to their several countries and free themselves from the yoke of Azcapotzalco. Then an alliance was created between the Mexicans and several other groups. Of these, by far the most important was the one which represented the ancient Chichimec dynasty that had reigned over Texcoco until Ixtlilxochitl's aforementioned defeat. The allies secured the neutrality of some of the Tepanec cities; and after an extremely difficult war, Azcapotzalco was taken in 1428. This did not bring the struggle to an end, for Maxtla took refuge in Coyoacán and in more distant places, until finally he was defeated definitively in 1433. Then, Netzahualcoyotl was able to return to Texcoco and begin the long reign which ended only with his death in 1472. The spoils of the conquered Tepanecs and their vast empire were divided among the three principal victors: Mexico, Texcoco, and Tacuba as leader of the Tepanec cities which had joined the side of the alliance.

In 1434 the triple alliance was formed, composed of these three cities that decided to unite forever, to conquer in common, and to divide the booty according to specified proportions. During Netzahualcoyotl's reign and due to his personal prestige, the alliance operated despite all; but upon his death, the Mexican lords gradually discarded their roles as simple members to become leaders of the alliance. In effect, at the time of the Spanish conquest the two of the former allies were at the point of becoming subjects of the third.

Because of the new state of things in the Valley of Mexico, the three powerful allies distributed the titles and ranks; Itzcoatl of Tenochtitlán appropriated the most distinguished title of all: "Culhuatecuhtli" meaning "Lord of the Culhuas." This name may seem strange at first sight. But we recall that Culhuacán, the capital of the Culhuas, was the place where the Toltec dynasty had been kept alive. Therefore, on adopting this title, Itzcoatl named himself Lord of the Toltecs and concluded in his favor the long "war of the Toltec succession." This at once meant that Mexico thought itself, from this moment on, the legitimate representative of the old culture and the heir, in every sense, of Toltec glory. For this reason the caciques of the Grijalva River, when first speaking of Mexico to Cortez, called it Culhua, something which quite naturally the Spaniards could not understand and, as Bernal Díaz said, "Since we did not know what Mexico was or our poorly pronounced version of Culhua, we overlooked the matter."

Once the Tepanec war was over and the power of Mexico was consolidated, Itzcoatl launched into new campaigns to establish his power over the cities which Tenochtitlán had formerly conquered when in the service of Azcapotzalco. So began the expansion beyond the Central Valleys which was to take them to such distant places.

In 1440, at the death of Itzcoatl, another great governor, Moctezuma I, his nephew, ascended to the throne and reigned until 1469. This new king consolidated the interior position of Tenochtitlán and it was at this moment that the Mexican empire was really constituted.

The wars of conquest began at once in different regions; they continued throughout his reign, reaching to Oaxaca

and the Gulf coast of Mexico. The conquest of the Totonacs, inhabitants of this latter region, was due in part
to one of those characteristic episodes in the history of
Tenochtitlán in which greed, patriotism, religion, and a
total lack of a sense of gratitude were mixed together. In
effect, between 1450 and 1454 an extreme and unusually
prolonged drought brought terrible hunger to the Mexicans. According to one of the sources, we are told that
even wild beasts came down from the mountains to attack
men and on the roads the dead were devoured by vultures.
To save themselves from this catastrophe the Mexicans resorted to two devices: on the one hand, they obtained
loans of corn from the Totonacs, and on the other, they
initiated an era of human sacrifices to an extent unheard
of until then in order to implore the favor of the gods.
When the crisis was past—I should say rather because of
Totonac corn than the spilled blood—Moctezuma I understood that the rich coastal lands were his best guarantee
against a new period of famine; and so, with his proverbial
gratitude, he dispatched troops to the coastal region. After
a succession of ferocious, surprise attacks, he conquered the
whole area and thereby permanently obtained the most important granary of ancient Mexico, which even today is
vital to Mexico's future.

The repeated and extensive triumphs of Moctezuma I
and the terror he managed to impose upon everybody tells
us that he practiced an unprecedented strategy of violence.
Like a virtual avalanche the Mexican troops fell upon the
peoples, broke down their disorganized resistance through
surprise attacks, captured their chief if that were possible,
mounted the temple and burned it. This was the signal
of victory and there was left only the work of dividing the
booty, women, and prisoners, establishing a government
submissive to Tenochtitlán, fixing the tribute, and marching off to a new conquest.

Between the battles and the war-shouts there was a brief
episode that recalls Alexander's victory over the Persians.
In about 1461 the Mexican troops conquered an important
domain—Coixtlahuaca—in the mountains of Oaxaca, and

after a great battle they gained victory and killed the lord. They brought the widow of the defeated leader to Mexico where Moctezuma immediately fell in love with her. She was a young woman of great beauty. But, like Darius' wife, she preferred to remain a prisoner with dignity than to marry her husband's conqueror.

The epic of Moctezuma I fortunately had some less tragic aspects, for while he was a great conqueror he was also a great builder. He brought in a group of architects from Chalco who were very famous. Thus began the transformation of the capital from a poor city of mud to a metropolis in stone (Plate 16). Not only was there an interest in architecture, but during his reign a great style of sculpture began, which had its own character and which has given us some of the most interesting monuments of Mexica art.

Among other things, he had his portrait engraved on the rock of Chapultepec, an example which his successors followed, thus creating a surprising gallery of Mexican kings, which time, unfortunately, has not respected. Only a few traces remain.

As a good Mexica, Moctezuma was also a lover of plants and flowers. In a rich valley of the Morelos region he created a botanical garden in which were plants taken from all different climates. The rarest and most beautiful flowers could be found there. His successors also were interested in botany and the magnificent gardens did not disappear until the end of the sixteenth century. In this region today they still show a garden which they call "Moctezuma's garden."

With the restoration of the Empire, the construction of the city, and the establishment of a religious pattern, it is very clear that Moctezuma I was the real forger of the Mexica empire. He invented practically nothing. But he reclaimed for his people, at last in power, the millenary heritage of all those who had preceded him. Huitzilopochtli was associated with the origin of this people. But in reality, he was only a small tribal god, an aspect of the god Tezcatlipoca, until his people's victories elevated him

to the rank of a god-creator. Then he became the sun itself, that is the giver of light, of heat, of the day and all
things necessary for life. But the sun, like every being created by the divine pair, needs nourishment, for he must
struggle daily against their enemies: the tigers of the night,
represented by the moon and the stars. We recall that this
is exactly what the infant Huitzilopochtli had to do when
he was born fully armed. But the sun, unfortunately for
the neighbors of the Mexica, could only be nourished with
the most precious of all victuals: the nectar of the gods,
that is, human blood. Then to keep it permanently alive
and to give it strength in its daily struggles, it was necessary to sacrifice human beings. The Mexica felt obliged
by their very history to be its guardians and sustainers. In
other words, it was their duty to provide the sun with human blood. This is, therefore, the excellent motive on an
indisputably high moral plane by which they claimed to
absolve themselves of all the wars and all the deaths. But
for their neighbors what a tragedy to live next to a chosen
people!

Some Indian regions of Mexico still retain a distant
memory of this idea by which man has the mission to defend the sun. I remember an incident a few years ago when
I was in a town near Acapulco. There was a partial eclipse
of the sun. The population at once came into the streets,
men, women, and children, armed with whatever object
was capable of making noise: musical instruments, empty
boxes, tables, old sheets of laminated metal, etc. The point
was to make so much noise that the tigers who were de-
vouring the sun would be frightened by the uproar and
leave. Let us be happy that now sound alone is enough
to carry out the task which before was performed with human hearts.

Even with all these data it is very difficult for us to understand what we might call the glory or desire of sacrifice.
For example, to what extent was the one who was being
sacrificed in agreement with his fate? On one hand, he
knew he was going to die. But on the other, he was to
be assimilated with the god, to become practically a divine

essence. We have contradictory data on this point. Outstanding warriors who had been taken prisoners and who were offered their lives did not accept so as to appear more courageous. They were sacrificed by their own choice. Then we hear about some groups, like the Tarasco prisoners, who managed to escape and had thereby cheated the gods who were counting on their blood. But we also hear of prisons in which the prisoners were guarded until the day of sacrifice and even bound so as not to escape. Although public opinion might criticize them and their own people might not wish to see them return, it is evident that many prisoners had the normal reaction to save their skin, and even run the risk that the god might be a little hungry.

It is obviously absurd to suppose, as many historians have stated, that the motives behind their wars were simply religious. War held out the promise of material advantages, conquests, booty, tributes, and a constant expansion of territorial boundaries. But the Mexicans were not the initiators nor the ones responsible for the "almost permanent state of war" in which they lived. We have seen how war had become an ever-present cultural trait from the very early times of Mixcoatl, and I believe since Olmec times. War is a social factor, a state of affairs. We see less of it at certain moments, as during the Teotihuacán period. But that succession of ephemeral empires and feudal lords forever up in arms shows a socio-political situation in which war was a "necessity." It was a situation which the Mexica inherited, as has unfortunately been the case in other periods and other places throughout human history.

What the Mexicans seem to have carried further than others is a religious sense of war. This is especially true in one of the most curious institutions known among any people: the "flowery war." We do not know when this custom really began, but by 1375 it already existed among the Tepanecs, from whom the Mexica probably inherited it. A "flowery war" takes place when two states agree to celebrate at a determined site and specific date a great battle whose only objective is to take prisoners alive. Whichever party wins acquires no territories from the other, does not sack the town, but simply carries prisoners off ready for sacrifice. They were therefore interested only in live ones, since the dead in battle were of no use whatsoever. A soldier rose in rank according to the number of prisoners he took, and he was authorized to wear special military decorations. In the wars of the Conquest, this idea saved the lives of many Spaniards, for the Indians wished to capture them alive, and as a result some prisoners escaped. Cortez himself, fallen and surrounded by enemies, managed to escape because instead of killing him they tried to carry him off alive.

Under Moctezuma I, probably because of the increasing need for victims, this custom was instituted between Tenochtitlán and some of the cities of the Valley of Puebla. In this way they did not have to go too far to find prisoners. But the obvious aftermath soon came about, that is, the Mexicans gradually were not satisfied with the simple selective war, and began a methodical conquest of great sections of the Puebla region, until at last the republic of Tlaxcala was tragically surrounded.

Meanwhile, Netzahualcoyotl was reigning over Texcoco. He had the good fortune to live many years, during which time he became the most famous monarch of his century. Apart from his multiple military victories and the continual enlargement of his reign, he succeeded in making his capital the intellectual center of his period. He was a great builder. Unfortunately, the vicissitudes through which Texcoco passed after his death have caused the total disappearance of the immense palaces which he built and the temples of his gods. The only material memory of this period is a pool, or rather a cistern, a part of an irrigation system situated in an admirable place among flowers and trees from which it dominated the landscape of the valley and the lakes. But Netzahualcoyotl's main glory did not stem from his buildings but from his influence on letters, laws, and religion. Himself a poet, he gathered to his court a select group of poetry and theater lovers, and as a result almost all Nahuatl literature we have either comes from the school of Texcoco or is strongly influenced by it.

His prestige as a legislator was so overwhelming that other cities copied his laws. Now they appear dreadful to us since capital punishment was applied to almost every crime, some of which were of minor importance to our way of thinking. Through these ordinances one can somewhat understand the Indian mentality and its concept of good and evil. Many of the laws were based on practical necessities; but others emanated from moral attitudes. They indicated an extraordinary rigidity, a true puritanism, in which, for example, any sexual sin as well as drunkenness were punished by death. At times, it was rather a matter of respecting taboos or magic ideas as in the horrible case of the hermaphrodite of Tlaxcala. Netzahualcoyotl himself applied his laws so rigorously that in one case he condemned one of his own sons to death for adultery. All this does not mean that the habits of the people were always so strict, and under the reign of his son they lost some of their severity.

Perhaps influenced by the old stories of Quetzalcoatl which were on everybody's lips, Netzahualcoyotl developed a much higher and purer religion. He believed in a supreme god, a simple incorporeal spirit of whom one could not make statues and who did not desire human sacrifices. This philosophical and abstract religion, in which there were no temples nor ceremonies, was not followed by the masses, who wanted more entertainment, and was preserved solely among a small elite of priests.

With Netzahuacoyotl's death began the decadence of Texcoco. His son, Netzahualpili, succeeded to the throne. He was called the "Fasting Prince"; he was a most curious figure, fully decadent and profoundly civilized.

* * * *

In 1469 Axayacatl took the throne of Tenochtitlán. Also a descendant of Acamapichtli, and as all the other Mexican kings, he launched a series of new conquests which expanded the territory of the empire. One important episode in the government of this lord was the conquest of the rival city Tlatelolco. From ancient times a city-state had been established here which for more than a century was considered allied to Tenochtitlán. Although increasingly dominated by Tenochtitlán, Tlatelolco retained at least an appearance of autonomy. For reasons of a political nature and even for personal motives, Axayacatl decided to bring to an end the independence of Tlatelolco. The king of this place had (undoubtedly for diplomatic reasons) married a sister of the lord of Mexico, " 'The Little Precious Stone,' whose teeth emitted a great stench, for which reason the king of Tlatelolco could never take pleasure in her. Her husband did not esteem her at all, for she was feeble, ugly, skinny, and fleshless and he deprived her of all the cotton blankets that Axayacatl sent her, and gave them to his concubines. The princess suffered very much, was obliged to sleep in a corner next to the wall, in the room where tortillas were made on the *metate*, and for herself she had only a coarse, ragged blanket. . . . Her husband lodged her in a different house from his concubines, he considered her of no value at all, and never wished to sleep with the princess, 'The Little Precious Stone,' and slept only with his concubines, who were graceful females."

This sad story of his sister soon reached the ears of Axayacatl; and using this personal insult as a pretext, he decided to carry out what his ambition dictated: the conquest of Tlatelolco. The struggle was intense and even the women valiantly defended the city. But at last it succumbed before the Mexica empire, whose soldiers mounted the great temple and from that height hurled down the king of Tlatelolco. With this the war was terminated in 1473.

Tlatelolco had close ties with the people of the Toluca Valley. Perhaps for this reason, when Tlatelolco fell, Axayacatl turned his attention to the conquest of all the cities in this region. In several of them are interesting ruins. But by far the most notable are those from the monolithic city of Malinalco. With a work plan that must have been carefully prepared beforehand, the masons cut out the soft stone, shaping a large, circular room with connecting stairways and sculptures. On the door was the face of an enormous serpent with its mouth open; on the sides were sculptures. On one side was a snake, with scales shaped like arrowheads, that served as a pedestal for a human figure. Unfortunately, only the feet have been left intact. The figure may have been an eagle-knight. On the other side was a jaguar-knight (also very incomplete today) that stood on a drum covered with jaguar skin. Beyond the door, one entered a circular room with a stone bench going around it. On the bench was depicted the skin of a jaguar consisting of the head, tail, and claws of the animal; on either side, and also on the bench, were two admirably made eagles; a third in the center completed the decoration. The conical roof must have been made of straw. All the elements of this building indicate that this was a place where were carried out the ceremonies of two military orders called Jaguar-knights and Eagle-knights. From what we know of these two orders, only the most famous warriors could belong to them. These two titles were conferred on them as very special honors. Curiously, like medieval orders, they combined a military spirit with religious obligations, which in the case of the Mexica were mainly directed to sun worship. We may deduce here that the temple of Malinalco was devoted to this same heavenly body.

Apart from the fine dexterity of the works—the slightest error was irreparable—aesthetically, these animal sculptures may be placed among the most beautiful examples of Mexica art. They have a very stylized yet realistic form in which a few lines suggest the qualities of the sculptured object much better than a most exact copy.

In one of the side rooms is preserved a fragment from a fresco depicting a file of walking warriors. Apart from its iconographic interest, this is one of the rarest painted murals in existence from this period; from the Valley of Mexico almost none are left.

As a result of conquests in the Valley of Toluca, the Mexicans found themselves adjacent to the great Tarascan kingdom. About 1480 began the inevitable war between

Fig. 21 Monkey in stone. Mexica sculpture. Drawing by A. Mendoza.

the two most important military powers of the moment. For the first time the Mexican tactics did not bring the usual results and their armies were defeated. From then on there was a curious kind of "cold war" between the rival kingdoms, and a "stone curtain" separated them, since both sides had built along the frontier a series of fortified points for defensive rather than offensive reasons. The Mexicans tried to hem in the enemy by conquering the

Fig. 22 Detail from a vessel. The monkey symbolizes happiness. Drawing by A. Mendoza.

entire Guerrero region so as to be able to attack the Tarascans also from the south. But this strategy did not work either, for they were never able to cross the Balsas River.

This threatening situation lasted until the Spanish conquest came and changed the balance of power. Perhaps because of the driving force of the Mexica soldiers, the Tarascans began to confront their enemy with superior arms, frequently made of copper.

The partial exploration of some of these fortresses has given us some information on the military art of the period. They were built on hills, hard to approach on all sides, protected by one or several circles of walls and at times by moats. They were defended by small garrisons of troops, but were not permanent towns. They maintained a strictly military character.

Axayacatl's government, apart from the aforesaid wars, was characterized by other wars in which the Mexica soldiers spread terror that grew from day to day. By this time the hatred which the Mexica empire inspired had taken

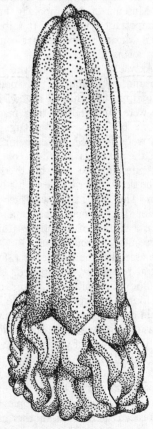

Fig. 23 Magnificent sculpture, Mexica culture, National Museum of Anthropology. Drawing by A. Mendoza.

root. This hatred was to be of prime importance when Cortez arrived on the scene.

In other aspects Axayacatl also followed the tradition of Moctezuma I. He built a large palace and continued the grand works of the main temple. From his period comes the great sculpture generally known as the Mexica calendar stone, and which in reality is a votive stone in honor of the sun. This monument, found today in Mexico's National Museum of Anthropology, has a rare perfection and an important symbolism. It initiated the period of monumental Mexica sculpture that continued through the succeeding reigns.

Following Axayacatl came Tizoc, who ruled only from 1481 to 1486 and, as it appears, was poisoned. Even in a short span of time he achieved a good many new conquests. These were immortalized in a magnificent monument: the stone of Tizoc. It is a large basalt cylinder around which were depicted the emperor's victories. The emperor wore the insignias and dress of Huitzilopochtli, for as a high priest of the god, his dress was identified with that of the deity. After his death his brother Ahuizotl succeeded him. The new leader was such a dreaded and brutal conqueror that his name has come down into even our own day as a symbol of something feared or of something that persecutes or troubles us.

The year he ascended the throne, in 1487, the construction of the great temple was completed. Ahuizotl decided to inaugurate the work with pomp and ceremony never dreamed of before. He went on a veritable hunt for prisoners and it is said that he proceeded to sacrifice eighty thousand men, as a result of which the sun undoubtedly gained new strength. The number of victims seems highly exaggerated. But whatever the toll of sacrifices may have been, it left an ineffaceable memory in the Indian mind.

The terror of the armies or the memory of the sacrifices convinced all the still unsubjugated peoples of the Mexican power. The Mexicans undertook another campaign in the south where they completed their conquests in Oaxaca and the Isthmus and reached the present-day frontier of Guate-

Fig. 24 The emperor Tizoc, attired as Huitzilopochtli, takes a prisoner. Detail from the stone of Tizoc. Drawing by A. Mendoza.

mala; the entire region of the Soconusco fell into their hands.

This great conqueror's death was not of the same magnitude as his deeds. In 1502 a broken dike caused a flood in Mexico City. While trying to escape, Ahuizotl smashed himself against the lintel of an archway and, like Charles VIII of France four years earlier, died as a result of this accident.

With his death ended the list of imposing military leaders who had ruled in Tenochtitlán since Moctezuma I and whose conquests had made the small city built on an island in the lake into the capital of a vast empire.

The organization of the armies, which were growing daily in importance; the management of the empire with all its political and economic problems; and even the adoption of urban life, which had disappeared several centuries before, all this was to transform profoundly the structure of the Mexica people. Now the small, nomadic, despised horde had become the ruling class and subduer of peoples as diverse as they were many. The old tribal system could not go on. The society was divided into classes, and there were nobles, plebeians, and slaves. Likewise there were merchants, priests, specialized workers in many manual skills, and an entire bureaucracy. This change is also noted in the person of the leader himself, who became more and more of an autocrat and who, as Moctezuma II, was transfigured into a kind of god. Like the Roman Caesars, power went to their heads, and the former organization turned increasingly into a kind of Oriental despotism.

When Moctezuma II was chosen emperor in 1502, he had the reputation of a valiant captain who had ably led his armies; but he was especially recognized as a profound expert in religious matters, a kind of simple and humble mystic. This situation rapidly changed as he became a despot at the center of highly intricate court ceremonies. No one was permitted to look upon him. One had to come before him with eyes lowered. No one could touch him. The few who had the right to visit him had to enter barefoot, performing a series of genuflections and calling him Lord, My Lord, My Great Lord.

The first seventeen years of his reign were spent in continual wars and in the suppression of rebellions by peoples who, desperate because of the suffocating oppression, rose in arms hoping vainly to escape the tributes which had been placed on them. But Moctezuma II took little personal part in all this. Rather, he lived in the city, devoted to his pleasures and religious duties. He was an intelligent and refined man, although profoundly superstitious, and his whole life was based on his beliefs. In 1519 the terrible news pierced the sky like a terrifying scream: Quetzalcoatl had returned. From the first moment Moctezuma knew that his reign was doomed, that the prophecies had been fulfilled, that struggle against a god was impossible. So he followed the only road left open, the only way to resist a god—by obtaining the aid of other gods and by attempting to convince Quetzalcoatl to depart.

On the one hand, he sent Cortez the insignias of his god: the plumed crest, the gold mask, and numerous gifts with which he hoped to convince him. These things convinced him, but of precisely the opposite. The gold simply reinforced his intention to continue the march.

On the other hand, Moctezuma gathered his priests and witch doctors from great distances, and embarked on a total campaign of magic against Cortez. As one may expect, the devices failed, one after another. The witch doctors were useless, and in complete disregard of Moctezuma's desperation, Cortez arrived one day before the gates of Mexico City.

For the last time, Moctezuma played his role as king and went out to receive the conquistador: "When we arrived near Mexico, where there were other small towers, the great Moctezuma got down from his litter, and those great caciques supported him with their arms, beneath a marvelously rich canopy of green-colored feathers with intricate patterns in gold and silver and with pearls and chalchuite emeralds hanging from a sort of embroidery, which was wonderful to behold. And the great Moctezuma was richly attired according to his practice, and he was shod with sandals, the soles were of gold and the upper part adorned with precious stones. And the four lords who supported his arms were also richly clothed according to their practice in garments which were apparently held ready for them on the road so that they might come out with their Lord, for they had not worn this attire when they first came out to receive us. And besides these four lords were four other great caciques who supported the canopy over their heads, and many other lords who walked before the great Moctezuma, sweeping the ground where he passed and placing blankets on the ground so that he would not tread on the earth. Not one of those lords dared even to think of looking directly at his face, but kept their eyes lowered with great awe, except for those four relations, his nephews, who supported him with their arms.

"And when Cortez saw and understood and when they told him that the great Moctezuma was coming, he got down from his horse, and as soon as he was near Moctezuma they simultaneously paid great reverence to each other. Moctezuma welcomed him and our Cortez replied through doña Marina wishing him very good health. And it seems to me that Cortez, through the tongue of doña Marina who was by his side, offered his right hand and Moctezuma did not wish to take it, but he did give his hand to Cortez. And then Cortez brought out a necklace which he had ready at hand, made of glass stones that I have already said are called *margaritas*, which contained intricate patterns and many colors, and the stones were strung on gold cords and with musk so that the necklace should have a sweet scent, and he strung it around the neck of the great Moctezuma, and when he had placed it there he was about to embrace him, and those great lords who accompanied Moctezuma held back the arm of Cortez so that he should not embrace him, for they considered it an indignity."

GLOSSARY—GAZETTEER—
PRONOUNCING GUIDE

ACAMAPICHTLI Ah-cah-mah-*peech*-tlee. First Mexica king, descendant of the Toltecs of Culhuacán.

ACAPULCO Ah-cah-*pool*-coh. "Place of the Reeds." Port and resort in the present state of Guerrero on the Pacific, southern Mexico.

ACHITOMETL Ah-chee-*toh*-mehtl. King of Culhuacán who gave lands in Tizapan to the Mexica at the beginning of the fourteenth century.

ACOLNAHUACATL Ah-cohl-nah-*wah*-cahtl. Proper name, inhabitant of Acolnahuac.

AHUITZOTL Ah-*weet*-sohtl. Mexica king of Tenochtitlán, ruled 1486–1502.

ALMIZCLE Ahl-*mees*-cleh. Musk.

ANAHUAC Ah-*nah*-wahk. "Next to the waters"; lake area of the Valley of Mexico; refers also to the coast regions.

APATZINGAN Ah-paht-seen-*gahn*. City in the present state of Michoacan, center of Tarascan culture.

AXAYACATL Ah-shah-*yah*-cahtl. Mexica king of Tenochtitlán, ruled 1469–1481.

AZCAPOTZALCO Ahs-cah-poh-*tsahl*-coh. Tepanec city northwest of Tenochtitlán, on the shore of Lake Texcoco, now part of Mexico City.

AZTEC See Mexica.

BALSAS *Bahl*-sahs. River that runs through the present state of Guerrero.

BONAMPAK Bohn-ahm-*pahk*. Classic Maya city (A.D. 300–900) found in the jungles of Chiapas in southeastern Mexico. Magnificent fresco paintings have been found in Bonampak.

CANDELARIA   Cahn-del-*ah*-ree-ah. Cave in Coahuila State not far from the city of Torreón. Important mummy bundle burials have been found here.

CE ACATL TOPILTZIN   Seh *Ah*-cahtl Toh-*peel*-tseen. "One Reed, Our Prince," name given to the son of Mix-coatl and Chimalman, born on a calendar day Ce Acatl in the Valley of Morelos. Topiltzin became ruler of the Toltecs and founder of the capital, Tula.

CERRO DE LAS MESAS   *Seh*-roh De Las *Meh*-sahs. Archae-ological zone of Olmec culture in Veracruz State where the largest cache of jade in Mesoamerica has been found, consisting of more than eight hundred pieces.

CHALCHIHUITES   Chahl-chee-*wee*-tehs. Archaeological zone in Zacatecas State.

CHALCO   *Chal*-coh. Lake town (on Lake Texcoco) south-east of Tenochtitlán.

CHAPULTEPEC   Chah-pool-teh-*pec*. "Grasshopper Hill," park which provided Tenochtitlán with potable wa-ter from its springs.

CHAYOTE   Cha-*yoh*-teh. Mexican vegetable, *Scisyos edulis*.

CHIA   *Chee*-ah. Lime-leaved sage. Used for making a soft drink.

CHICHEN ITZA   Chee-*chen* Eet-*sah*. "Mouth of the well of the Itzaes," great Maya metropolis that flourished from Classic times (ca. A.D. 300) to the fifteenth century; in the later period it was the home of the Itzá dynasty. Found west of Mérida in Yucatan.

CHICHIMEC   *Chee*-chee-mehk. "Dog lineage," tribal name given to the hordes of Xolotl. Chichimec also means nomad.

CHIMALMAN   Chee-*mahl*-mahn. "Shield hand," wife of Mixcoatl and mother of Topiltzin-Quetzalcoatl— Toltec culture hero and founder of the capital, Tula.

CHIMALPOPOCA   Chee-mahl-poh-*poh*-cah. Mexica king of Tenochtitlán from 1417–1427.

CHOLULA   Choh-*loo*-lah. Large commercial and religious

center in the present state of Puebla, flourished during the Classic and Postclassic periods (ca. A.D. 300–1200), existed at the time of the Spanish conquest in 1519–21. Its pyramid is said to be the largest in the world in terms of cubic feet.

CIUDADELA   See-oo-dah-*deh*-lah. Stadium in Teotihuacán, in which stands the Temple of Quetzalcoatl.

COATEPANTLI   Coh-ah-teh-*pan*-tlee. "Serpent wall," enclosure where the wall is decorated with reliefs of serpents.

COATL   *Coh*-ah-tl. Snake in Nahuatl, language of the Mexica.

COHUATZIN   Coh-*wah*-tseen. Interpreter. Proper name, "Little Snake."

COLHUACAN   Col-*wah*-can. Culhuacán.

COMAL   Coh-*mahl*. Flat earthenware pan for cooking tortillas (maize cakes).

COPIL   *Coh*-peel. Nephew of Huitzilopochtli.

COPILCO   Coh-*peel*-coh. Preclassic (ca. 2000–150 B.C.) site south of Tenochtitlán, now in the Villa Obregón suburb of Mexico City.

CORTEZ   Cohr-*tes*. Hernán Cortez, Spanish conqueror of Mexico; conquest realized in 1521.

CU   *Koo*. Temple.

CUERNAVACA   Cwer-nah-*vah*-cah. Spanish corruption of the preconquest Cuauhnahuac ("Next to the trees," or Forest), now capital of the state of Morelos.

CUICUILCO   Cwee-*cweel*-coh. Preclassic (ca. 2000–150 B.C.) site in the Valley of Mexico, south of Tenochtitlán, next to the present University City.

CULHUACAN   Cool-wah-*cahn*. First Toltec capital, established by Mixcoatl at the foot of Star Hill, south of Tenochtitlán.

CULHUATECUHTLI   Cool-wah-te-*coo*-tlee. "Lord of the Culhuas," or Toltec descendant, title given himself by Itzcoatl, fourth king of the Tenochtitlán Mexica.

DURANGO   Door-*ahn*-goh. State in northern Mexico.

GRIJALVA   Gree-*hahl*-vah. River in Chiapas State, southern Mexico, named for sixteenth-century Spanish explorer who penetrated this area.

GUALUPITA   Gwah-loo-*pee*-tah. Preclassic (ca. 2000–150 B.C.) site in present-day Cuernavaca, Morelos State.

GUASAVE   Gwah-*sah*-veh. Archaeological zone in Sinaloa State.

GUERRERO   Geh-*re*-roh. State in southern Mexico. Acapulco is perhaps its best-known city today.

HUASTECA   Wahs-*teh*-cah. Region in northeastern Mexico.

HUAUHTLI   W*ah*-oo-tlee. Mosquito-egg "caviar" removed from the surface of Lake Texcoco's water, still eaten today.

HUEHUETEOTL   Weh-weh-*teh*-ohtl. "Old God," deity of Fire.

HUEMAC   W*eh*-mahc. Last Toltec king who reigned in Tula; his reign ended in 1168. Huemac means "Big Hand."

HUITZILIHUITL   Wee-tsee-*lee*-weetl. Second Mexica king, reigned 1396–1417.

HUITZILOPOCHTLI   Wee-tsee-loh-*pohtch*-tlee. War God, principal deity of the Mexica. In legend, son of Coatlicue, mother of the gods; also son of the two original Creators, Ometecuhtli and Omecihuatl.

ICXICOUATL   Eek-shee-*coh*-watl. Toltec-Chichimec historical hero.

IPALNEMOANI   Ee-pahl-neh-moh-*ah*-nee. Lord of the World, all-powerful invisible god.

IXTLILXOCHITL   Eesh-tleel-*shoh*-cheetl. King of Texcoco, reigned 1409–1418; father of Netzahualcoyotl.

ITZCOATL   Ees-*coh*-ahtl. Mexica king of Tenochtitlán who ruled from 1427–1440.

JALISCO   Hahl-*ees*-coh. State in western Mexico, part of which is bordered by the Pacific Ocean.

KAMINALJUYU   Kah-meen-ahl-hoo-*yoo*. Classic (ca. A.D. 300–900) Maya city in Guatemala.

KUKULCAN   Koo-kool-*kahn*. Feathered serpent, name for Quetzalcoatl in Maya.

LA VENTA   Lah V*en*-tah. Olmec site in Tabasco State from Preclassic period (ca. 2000–150 B.C.)

renowned for its magnificent jade figurines and colossal heads of basalt stone.

MANO *Mah*-noh. Long, cylindrical stone for grinding on the *metate*.

MAXTLA *Mahsh*-tlah. Son of Tezozomoc, the tyrant of Azcapotzalco. He succeeded to the throne when his father died in 1426 by having his brother murdered.

MESOAMERICA *Me*-soh-America. Middle America, term used by Kirchhoff to designate the region comprehended between the northern border of present-day Mexico and the southern border of Central America.

METATE Me-*tah*-teh. Flat, long grinding stone, used mainly for grinding corn.

MEXICA Dominating group in the Valley of Mexico at the time of the Spanish conquest (A.D. 1519–1521). Founders of Tenochtitlán and Tlatelolco in the fourteenth century; empire builders par excellence. The name Aztec comes from Aztlan or Aztatlan, Place of the Herons, place of origin of these people, located in Nayarit or Jalisco.

MEXICO Meh-*shee*-coh is the correct pronunciation but today *Mex*-ee-coh is used. "Place of Huitzilopochtli" or "Place in the center of the moon."

MEZQUITAL Mes-kee-*tahl*. Valley in the present state of Hidalgo, area from where Xolotl came with his hordes to invade the Valley of Mexico.

MICAOTLI Mee-cah-*oh*-tlee. "Street of the Dead," name given in period of later occupation to a great central avenue in Teotihuacán.

MICHOACAN Mee-choh-ah-*cahn*. "Place of fish," region of Tarascan culture. Present state of this name in midwestern Mexico.

MIXCOATL Meesh-*coh*-ahtl. Chieftain of the Toltecs at the time of their arrival in the Valley of Mexico in a barbarian state (ca. A.D. 900). Father of Topiltzin, founder of Tula and the great culture hero. Mixcoatl was deified by Topiltzin and worshiped as a god from then on.

MIXTECA Mees-*teh*-cah. Region in Oaxaca, home of a
highly developed prehispanic culture that has left
us many important documents (codices).

MOCTEZUMA Mohc-teh-*soo*-mah. Two Mexica-Tenochti-
tlán kings: the first, Moctezuma Ilhuicamina (I),
ruled 1440–1469; the second, Moctezuma Xocoyo-
tzin (II), 1502–1520.

MOLCAJETE Mohl-cah-*he*-teh. Round grinding stone in
the form of a bowl, smaller than the *metate*. Used
generally for grinding chilis, tomatoes, etc.

MONTE ALBÁN *Mohn*-tay Ahl-*bahn*. Important Classic city
(A.D. 300–900) but with earlier occupation, located
on a hill south of Oaxaca City in the state of Oaxaca, southern Mexico. Most of its buildings were
constructed by the Zapotecs. Monte Albán's famed
jewels are of Mixtec manufacture.

MORELIA Mohr-*eh*-lee-ah. Capital of the state of Michoacan in midwestern Mexico.

MORELOS Mohr-*ay*-loes. State in Central Mexico, south of
Mexico City. Site of preconquest cultures such as
the Tlahuica. Xochicalco, Teopanzolco, Tepoztlan,
and other preconquest centers are found in Morelos.

NAHUATL *Nah*-wahtl. Language of the Mexica, of the
Yuto-Aztecan family.

NETZAHUALCOYOTL Nets-ah-wahl-*coy*-ohtl. Poet-prince of
Texcoco, ally of the Mexica of Tenochtitlán.

NIXTAMAL Nees-tah-*mahl*. Dough of corn and lime, with
which tortillas are made.

NONOHUALCAS Nohn-oh-*ahl*-cahs. Group of people who
lived in Tula with the Toltecs but who spoke another language at the beginning. The Nonohualcas
were excellent artisans; it seems that they were
taken to Tula by Topiltzin. The name means
"those of a foreign tongue" or "dumb."

OAXACA Wah-*hah*-cah. Valley in the present state of the
same name. Region where important preconquest
cities such as Monte Albán, Mitla, Zaachila, and

Yagul are found. Originally *Huaxyacac* (Wah-shee-*ah*-cahc).

OCELOPAN   Oh-say-*loh*-pahn. Proper name, "Ocelot banner."

OLMEC   *Ohl*-mec. Vigorous culture that flourished between 2000–150 B.C., produced magnificent works of sculpture and lapidary and probably invented the calendar system used by the Mayas.

PAPALOAPAN   Pah-pah-loh-*ah*-pahn. "Place of Butterflies," river and basin of this name in the state of Veracruz, eastern Mexico.

PIPIL   Pee-*peel*. Dialect of the Nahuatl language spoken principally in Central America. Ethnic group in El Salvador.

POPOCATEPETL   Poh-poh-cah-*teh*-petl. "Smoking mountain." Snow-capped extinguished volcano between the valleys of Mexico and Puebla, clearly visible from Tenochtitlán.

PULQUE   Pool-keh. Principal Mexican alcoholic drink in preconquest times, still the national drink in central Mexico. Made from the liquid removed from the heart of the maguey (agave) cactus.

QUEMADA, LA   Keh-*mah*-dah. Archaeological ruins in the state of Zacatecas, in northern Mexico.

QUERETARO   Keh-*reh*-tah-roh. State in central Mexico.

QUETZAL   Ket-*sahl*. Bird whose plumage was highly valued in preconquest Mexico; found in Guatemala.

QUETZALCALLI   Ket-sahl-*cah*-lee. "House of Feathers," the quetzal bird being that which produced the most beautiful ones.

QUETZALCOATL   Ket-sahl-*coh*-ahtl. Deity, Bringer of Civilization, early god of flowing water, represented as a feathered serpent. Later viewed as Wind God by the Mexica, also called Ehecatl. Quetzalcoatl was also the name given to certain high priests.

QUETZALTEHUEYAC   Ket-sahl-teh-*weh*-yahc. Toltec-Chichimec personage.

QUINAMETZIN   Keen-ah-*met*-seen.   Giants,   supposedly builders of the majestic Teotihuacán. This confusion existed because bones of ancient mammoths were found frequently in the area.

SAN LORENZO   Olmec site from the Preclassic period (ca. 2000–150 B.C.) in southern Veracruz State.

SOCONUSCO   Soh-coh-*noos*-coh. Region in Chiapas in southern Mexico.

TAJIN   Tah-*heen*. Classic (ca. A.D. 300–900) Totonac city in what is now Veracruz State.

TARASCANS   Tah-*ras*-cans. Ethnic group from Michoacan in midwest Mexico, enemies of the Mexica.

TEAYO   Teh-*ah*-yoh. Archaeological zone in Veracruz State; Mexica outpost in zone of Totonac culture.

TECPANCALTZIN   Tec-pahn-*cahl*-tseen. One of the Toltec kings of Tula.

TENAYUCA   Ten-ah-*yoo*-cah. Chichimec city now on the northwestern outskirts of Mexico City. Its pyramid served as the model for Tenochtitlán's Great Temple.

TENOCH   *Ten*-och. Semi-legendary priest connected with the founding of Tenochtitlán.

TENOCHTITLÁN   Ten-och-*tee*-tlahn. Mexica capital whose beginnings were constructed on an island in Lake Texcoco, Valley of Mexico, now Mexico City. Tenochtitlán means "next to the prickly pear cactus."

TEOTIHUACÁN   Teh-oh-tee-wah-*cahn*. "Place of the gods." Great ceremonial center in central Mexico, the lifespan of which covered ca. 200 B.C.–A.D. 800.

TEOTLALPAN   Teh-oh-*tlahl*-pahn. Area immediately north of Mexico City, land of Otomí and Chichimec peoples. "Land of the gods" or of "authentic peoples."

TEPANECA   Teh-pah-*ne*-cah. One of the ethnic groups that arrived in the central region of Mexico about the same time as the Mexica, in the thirteenth century A.D. Later, inhabitants of Azcapotzalco, city on the shores of Lake Texcoco, west of Tenochtitlán.

TEPANTITLA   Teh-pahn-*teet*-lah. Section of Teotihuacán, where the frescoes of Tlalocan are found.

TEPEXPAN   Teh-*pesh*-pahn. Site northeast of Tenochtitlán,

near the Teotihuacán pyramids, where "Tepexpan Man," a hunter from about ten thousand years ago, was discovered, associated with implements.

TEPOZTLAN Teh-pohs-*tlahn*. Town east of Cuernavaca, in the state of Morelos. Birthplace of Ce Acatl Topiltzin.

TESONTLI Teh-*sohn*-tlee. Reddish volcanic stone.

TEXCOCO Tes-*coh*-coh. Town northeast of Tenochtitlán, home of the famed poet-prince Netzahualcoyotl. Also Lake Texcoco, which covered all of the Valley of Mexico at one time, and is now almost completely dry.

TEZCATLIPOCA Tehs-cah-tlee-*poh*-cah. Eagle God, representing the Sun. In the Mexica period, the deity who carried a mirror through which he observed deeds of men on earth and punished them accordingly. He demanded human sacrifices in his honor. There were four Tezcatlipocas, indicating the four cardinal directions.

TEZOZOMOC Te-soh-*soh*-mohc. King of Azcapotzalco, reigned 1363–1426. Under his leadership Azcapotzalco became the most important city in the Valley of Mexico at that time and head of a great incipient empire.

TEZOZOMOCTLI Teh-soh-soh-*mohc*-tlee. Proper name, nobleman important in the early Mexica period.

TICOMAN Tee-coh-*mahn*. Site north of Tenochtitlán, dating from the Preclassic period (ca. 2000–150 B.C.), formerly on the shores of Lake Texcoco.

TILANTONGO Teel-ahn-*tohn*-goh. One of the capitals of the Mixtec people, in northern Oaxaca.

TIZAPAN Tee-sah-*pahn*. Town at the southern extreme of what is now Mexico City, where the Mexica lived before settling Tenochtitlán.

TIZOC *Tee*-sohc. Mexica king of Tenochtitlán, ruled 1481–1486.

TLACATECUHTLI Tlah-cah-teh-*cu*-tlee. Military leader, one

of Moctezuma's functions together with civil duties.

TLACHIUHTETELLI   Tlahch-chee-oo-teh-*tel*-ee.   Man-made mound.

TLALMOMOZTLI   Tlahl-moh-*mohs*-tlee. Pyramid of earth.

TLALOC   *Tlah*-lohc. Rain God, worshiped from times of Teotihuacán (ca. beginning of the Christian era), later adopted by other peoples, including the Mexica.

TLALOCAN   Tlah-*loh*-cahn. Heaven dedicated to Tlaloc, Rain God, portrayed in frescoes in Tepantitla, Teotihuacán; from the Classic period (A.D. 300–900).

TLATELOLCO   Tlah-te-*lohl*-coh. "Artificial mound of sand": sandy pyramid. Twin Mexica city with Tenochtitlán on Lake Texcoco; while Tenochtitlán was the great religious-ceremonial-civil center, Tlatelolco was the important market, or commercial center.

TLATILCO   Tlah-*teel*-coh. Preclassic (ca. 2000–150 B.C.) site west of Tenochtitlán.

TLAXCALA   Tlahs-*cah*-lah. Region east of Tenochtitlán; its inhabitants were strong enemies of the Mexica at the time of the Spanish conquest, and therefore became allies of the Europeans.

TLOTZIN   *Tloh*-tseen. Grandson of Xolotl, Chichimec chieftain. "Little Hawk."

TOHUEYO   Toh-*beh*-yoh. Huastec vegetable vendor who married the daughter of Huemac, last Toltec king and enemy of the Huastecs.

TOLTEC   *Tohl*-tec. Postclassic culture (ca. A.D. 900–1250); its capital was in Tula, now in the state of Hidalgo.

TOLUCA   Toh-*loo*-cah. City in Mexico State west of Mexico City (Tenochtitlán), in the valley of the same name. Inhabited by Matlatzincas, and later Mexica, in preconquest times.

TORREON   Toh-reh-*ohn*. Modern city in Coahuila State, in western Mexico.

TORTILLA   Tohr-*tee*-yah. Thin corn cake like pancake in shape, the bread of ancient and modern Mexico.

TRES ZAPOTES   Tres Sah-*poh*-tehs. Olmec site in Veracruz State where the oldest known date in Maya style glyphs, corresponding to 31 B.C., has been found.

TULA   *Too*-lah. Capital of Toltec empire, situated in the present state of Hidalgo, north of Mexico City. Postclassic site that flourished from A.D. 900 to 1200.

UAXACTUN   Wah-shahc-*toon*. City in the Peten region of Guatemala, where one of the oldest Maya pyramids, E-VII-Sub, is found.

VERACRUZ   Vehr-ah-*croos*. State in eastern Mexico, limited by the Gulf of Mexico.

XALTOCAN   Shal-*toh*-cahn. Island city in the northern part of Lake Texcoco, called Xaltocan Lake here. "Sandspider place."

XAMANTUN   Shah-mahn-*toon*. Ancient Maya city in Yucatán.

XIPE   *Shee*-peh. God of Spring, "Our Lord the flayed one"; his priests dressed in the skin of the sacrificed victim.

XITLE   *Shee*-tleh. Now extinct volcano that erupted in archaic times and covered the southern part of the Valley of Mexico, causing the formation of the Pedregal or extension of petrified lava.

XOCHICALCO   Soh-chee-*cahl*-coh. Classic center (A.D. 300–900) in the present state of Morelos. City connected with the cult to Quetzalcoatl. "Flowery House."

XOCHIMILCO   Soh-chee-*meel*-coh. Town south of Mexico City, built mainly of *chinampas* (islands made of lake mud and reeds which later took root); now referred to as the "Floating Gardens."

XOLOTL   *Shoh*-loh-tl. Chieftain of the Chichimecs who invaded the Valley of Mexico in A.D. 1224.

XULTUN   Shool-*toon*. Ancient Maya site.

ZACATECAS   Sah-cah-*teh*-cas. State in Mexico in the northwestern region.

ZACATENCO Sah-cah-*ten*-coh. Preclassic (ca. 2000–150
     B.C.) site north of Tenochtitlán, near Ticomán,
     formerly on the shore of Lake Texcoco (now al-
     most dry).